═ ICONIC ═

CHICAGO

Dishes, Drinks and Desserts

D0779573

AMY BIZZARRI

AMERICAN PALATE

Contents

INTRODUCTION

Chicago is a city of big shoulders and big appetites. Our city's iconic dishes, desserts and drinks reflect our history as the "hog butcher of the world," "stacker of wheat" and "player with railroads and the nation's freight handler." Scraps of meat were transformed into dishes altogether sublime, breads and cakes sustained and sweetened lives, rail cars shipped meat to the East Coast and came back packed with the fruits of the ocean. Our rich immigrant history altered and expanded our taste buds.

Former mayor Richard J. Daley described Chicago as the "city that works," and the food that fuels a Chicago workday needs to be hearty and filling, portable, inexpensive and belly warming enough to sustain us through our cold winter days. The recipes featured herein recall our city's hard-at-work history, as well as the restaurants, bakeries, taverns and humble pushcarts that were loved by our great-grandparents, grandparents and parents. If we're lucky, they'll be cherished by our children, too. These are the iconic dishes, desserts and drinks that shaped the food landscape in Chicago, defining not just food history but also the history of the people who call this windy, wonderful city home.

BERTHA PALMER'S BROWNIES

If Chicago had royalty, Bertha Palmer would be considered one of the most generous queens in city history. Intelligent, inventive and beautiful, she bestowed her charm and grace on a gritty city on the move. Born in 1849 in Louisville, Kentucky, with a silver spoon in her mouth, she was so striking that Chicago retail and real estate magnate Potter Palmer, rendered instantly dumbstruck the first time he met her, waited until she came of age, in 1870, to marry her. Historian Ernest Poole described her best when he said, "She was beautiful, dashing, quick, and smart; and more than that, she was sure of herself."

But Bertha Palmer was not a mere socialite, content with living the gilded life in a rapidly growing Chicago. When Potter Palmer's Palmer House Hotel—a wedding gift to Bertha—burned to the ground in the Great Chicago Fire of 1871, she supported her husband as he rebuilt his fortune from the ashes. She played a key role in the city's social and cultural development and was an early member of the politically active Chicago Woman's Club. Bertha Palmer voiced her support of universal kindergarten as an integral part of the Chicago school system. She campaigned for basic women's rights, including subsidized milk for impoverished children and better care for the children of imprisoned mothers. As president of the board of lady managers for the World's Columbian Exposition, she worked to ensure that women were well represented in both the Women's Building and beyond; her first step was her insistence that a competition—open to women only—be held to select the architect of the Woman's Building. She

You'll find Bertha Palmer's original brownie at the historic Palmer House Hilton, Chicago. *Image courtesy of the Palmer House Hilton, Chicago.*

was a savvy patron of the arts, collecting a number of French impressionist works, now the central masterpieces of the Art Institute of Chicago's collection. At the World's Columbian Exposition of 1893 dedication ceremony, Bertha remarked, "Even more important than the discovery of Columbus, which we are gathered together to celebrate, is the fact that the general government has just discovered women."

Many people don't know that this grand dame invented one of America's tastiest treats: the brownie. During the 1893 exposition, Bertha Palmer worked with the Palmer House pastry chef to create a delicious dessert that would be compact enough to fit into a boxed lunch for attending ladies. Smart, stylish ladies need not worry about crumbs landing in their laps. The result was the rich, chocolaty, yet petite and less crumbly brownie, a small square that was big on taste yet offered a more elegant eating experience for ladies on the move.

The Palmer House still sticks to the original, rich and chocolaty brownie recipe, which calls for more than a pound of melted, top-quality chocolate; a pound of melted butter; and an apricot jelly glaze. The best place to enjoy Bertha's brownie is in the ever-sublime Lobby Bar in the Palmer House Hilton, which remains one of the most historic and stunning hotel lobbies in the world.

Bertha Palmer's Brownies

14 ounces semi-sweet chocolate
1 pound butter
12 ounces granulated sugar
4 ounces flour
8 eggs
Vanilla extract
12 ounces crushed walnuts

Preheat oven to 300° Fahrenheit. Melt chocolate and butter in a double boiler. Mix sugar and flour together in a bowl. Combine chocolate and flour mixtures. Stir 4 to 5 minutes. Add eggs and vanilla extract and continue mixing.

Pour mixture into a 9 x 12 baking sheet. Sprinkle walnuts on top, pressing down slightly into the mixture with your hand. Bake for 30 to 40 minutes. Brownies are done when the edges begin to crisp and have risen about ¼ of an inch.

Note: when brownie is properly baked, it will remain "gooey" with a toothpick in the middle due to the richness of the mixture.

Glaze

1 cup water
1 cup apricot preserves
1 teaspoon unflavored gelatin

Mix together water, preserves and unflavored gelatin in a saucepan. Mix thoroughly and bring to a boil for 2 minutes. Brush hot glaze on brownies while still warm.

Recipe courtesy of the Palmer House Hilton Hotel, Chicago

CHICAGO-STYLE GIARDINIERA

Giardiniera is Chicago's most celebrated condiment. Tangy, spicy and sweet, it cuts the richness of its best friend, the Italian beef sandwich, adding an extra element of crunch. Though it should be pronounced "Jar-Din-Air-Ah," true Chicagoans cut off that last "Ah" syllable.

While sottoaceti, pickled and canned veggies, are common in Italy, Chicago was the first to concoct a sottoaceti recipe of its very own. "Here in Chicago, we up the ante, adding more chilies and skipping a few of the ingredients found in a traditional Italian sottoaceti," shares Chicago-based foodie John Amici.

> *The result is more condiment than antipasto, and it's a staple of most "reputable" sandwich shops. In fact, in some circles, it's almost sacrilege to order an Italian beef sandwich without a healthy scoop of giardiniera to top it off. Good giardiniera also makes a great topping for any sandwich, as well as for burgers, hot dogs and brats, while a healthy sprinkling of it can elevate even the most lackluster of pizzas.*

"In reality, the hardest part of this recipe is to determine an acceptable level of heat," notes Amici.

> *After all, one person's idea of mildly spicy is another's five-alarm fire. I've learned through experimentation that four whole jalapeños, along with four that have been seeded and "de-ribbed," deliver just the right*

Chicago-Style Giardiniera sets itself apart from other sottoaceti with the addition of hot peppers. *John Amici.*

Chicago-Style Giardiniera: the ultimate condiment for a Chicago-style Italian beef sandwich. *John Amici.*

amount of heat for my palate. You, however, may prefer it hotter, so, follow the recipe and use eight whole jalapeños. If that still doesn't do it for you, switch out some or all of the jalapeños for serranos. On the other side of the coin, some may want their giardiniera mild, with very little heat, if any. By removing the jalapenos' ribs and seeds, you'll get a mild giardiniera that includes the flavor of jalapeños but none of the heat. And if that's not mild enough, drop the red pepper flakes. The point is, you can make the giardiniera as hot, or mild, as you like. With a little experimentation, you'll discover the right combination of chilies and pepper flakes to create the perfect giardiniera.

Chicago-Style Giardiniera

8 jalapeños, chopped (for more heat, serranos may be
   substituted)
½ large cauliflower, cut into florets
2 carrots, diced
2 celery stalks, diced
1 green bell pepper, diced
1 red bell pepper, diced
2 sweet banana peppers, diced
1 sweet onion, diced
½ cup kosher salt
3 cloves garlic, minced
2½ teaspoons dried oregano
1 teaspoon red pepper flakes
½ teaspoon celery seeds
Black pepper, to taste
½ cup cider vinegar
¼ cup white vinegar
½ cup extra virgin olive oil
½ cup vegetable/canola oil

Combine vegetables and salt. Add enough water to cover, stir, cover and refrigerate for at least 12 hours. Strain vegetables from brine, rinse well and set aside.

In a large glass bowl, add garlic and seasonings. Add the vinegars and oils and stir until well combined. Add the reserved, brined vegetables.

At this point, the giardiniera may be left, covered, in the bowl or transferred to clean jars. Either way, it must be refrigerated for 48 hours before serving. Because this giardiniera isn't canned, it must be stored in the refrigerator, where it will keep for two weeks.

Recipe courtesy of John Amici, fromthebartolinikitchens.com

BLACKHAWK SPINNING SALAD

From 1952 until closing day in 1984, waiters at the Blackhawk in Chicago were required to elegantly twirl an aluminum salad bowl over a bed of crushed ice, tableside. As they tossed the greens and added the dressing to the iconic Spinning Salad, they delivered a memorized spiel:

> *This is our famous Blackhawk spinning salad bowl consisting of twenty-one ingredients, including a variety of fresh pulled greens. First we spin the bowl and apply the basic dressing. Next we add a bit of special seasoning, and then some chopped egg. We mix the salad a total of six times only, very gently, three now and three times later, in order not to bruise the tender greens. Next we add some freshly ground pepper and our special blue cheese dressing. We now mix the salad three more times. And serve—topped with anchovies or shrimp.*

The Blackhawk, which opened its doors at 139 North Wabash in 1920, wasn't your everyday restaurant: it was a place to see, be seen and swing to the big band beat. An orchestra, Carlton Coon-Joe Sanders and their Kansas City Nighthawks, the first Kansas City jazz band to achieve national recognition, kept the crowds on their dancin' toes. Anyone who couldn't make it to the Blackhawk that evening could tune in at home: music from the Blackhawk was broadcast nationally as *Live! From the Blackhawk!* and locally on WGN Radio. Jazz great Mel Torme performed his first paying gig onstage at the Blackhawk in 1929. In 1938, Bob Haggart, one of the finest rhythm bassists of the swing era, composed "Big Noise from Winnetka" with drummer Ray Bauduc at the Blackhawk. Doris Day, who began her career as a big band singer, made her debut at the Blackhawk. Even the waiters attained celebrity status. The live Blackhawk broadcasts were so popular that a telegraph machine took in requests from afar.

As times and tastes changed, owner Don Roth stopped featuring orchestras in 1952, removing both the bandstand and the dance floor, and changed the restaurant's mission statement to "The Food's the Show." Prime rib, served tableside, and the spinning salad bowl became the Blackhawk's latest showstoppers.

The Blackhawk closed in 1984, and the only way to enjoy a Spinning Salad today is from the comfort of home. Though Roth likely copied the spinning salad bowl concept from the original Lawry's in Beverly Hills, he is credited with creating a recipe exclusive to the Blackhawk. Place the salad in an aluminum bowl set over a larger bowl filled halfway with crushed ice and dazzle your guests as you simultaneously spin the bowl and drizzle on the dressing.

Blackhawk Spinning Salad

Salad Dressing
1 (3-ounce) package cream cheese, softened
3 ounces blue cheese, crumbled
¼ cup water
¼ cup lemon juice
1 cup vegetable oil, divided
¼ cup red wine vinegar
2 teaspoons Worcestershire sauce
1 teaspoon prepared mustard
1 teaspoon paprika
1 teaspoon seasoned salt
1 teaspoon garlic powder
1 teaspoon ground white pepper
1 tablespoon granulated sugar
3 drops Tabasco sauce
2 tablespoons chives, chopped

Salad

1 small head iceberg lettuce, chopped
1 small head romaine lettuce, chopped
1 small head endive, chopped
12 cherry tomatoes
1 hard-boiled egg, peeled and crumbled
8 anchovy fillets
Black pepper to taste

Add the dressing ingredients—excluding the chives—to a food processor and blend until smooth. Add the chives and pulse 3 times.

In a salad bowl, mix the chopped iceberg, romaine, endive and tomatoes. Place the salad in an aluminum bowl set over a larger bowl filled halfway with crushed ice and dazzle your guests as you simultaneously spin the bowl and drizzle on the dressing.

Garnish with chopped egg, anchovies and freshly ground black pepper to taste.

BERGHOFF CREAMED SPINACH

As with many Chicago innovations, the World's Columbian Exposition of 1893 played a key role in the founding of the Berghoff. Herman Berghoff, an immigrant to America from Dortmund, Germany, sold his family-brewed beer from a tent just outside the fairgrounds. Herman liked bustling Chicago, and since his Berghoff Beer was a hit at the exposition, he decided to open up a men's only saloon where he continued to offer his winning world's fair deal. A glass of Dortmunder-style beer cost just a nickel and came with a free sandwich—corned beef, boiled ham or frankfurter—with a hard-boiled egg and a pickle on the side. A small note in the 1898 end-of-the-year *Chicago Daily Tribune* reported that Herman Berghoff's brewing company of Fort Wayne, Indiana, paid $175,000 to rent a building at the corner of State and Adams Streets for five years.

By 1914, the Berghoff had morphed from a saloon to a full-service restaurant at 17 West Adams. The hearty, German-inspired cuisine—including kassler rippchen (smoked Thüringer and bratwurst in sauerkraut topped with a smoked pork chop), creamed herring, Lyonnais potatoes, Wiener schnitzel, sauerbraten (marinated then roasted sirloin of beef topped with a sweet and sour gravy), apple strudel and creamed spinach—soon drew patrons just as much as the excellent draft beer. All of the original favorites are still on the menu today, along with a more contemporary twist on the old German classics. You'll still find Berghoff's original draft lager on tap—available today in amber, dark or seasonal varieties—as well as Berghoff Hefe Weizen, a smooth, Bavarian-style wheat beer;

the light, copper-colored, medium-bodied Berghoff Pale Ale; the deep mahogany Berghoff Dark; and Berghoff Amber Stein, a reddish-copper pale ale. Berghoff's crusty and hearty rye bread is still served in every bread basket.

When the iconic Berghoff threatened to close its doors forever in 2005, Chicago legend Studs Terkel summed up its importance: "The Berghoff seems to be one of the connecting links to the early Chicago that's still healthy, good and meant what it said—good food and service." The establishment managed not only to survive but also now thrives in the hands of a fourth-generation daughter, Carolyn Berghoff, making the Berghoff one of the oldest family-run businesses in the nation. Creamed spinach remains the Berghoff's single most popular side dish since it was introduced by executive chef Karl Hertenstein in 1945. Many have tried to re-create the secret recipe, but here's the real deal, shared by Carolyn Berghoff herself.

Berghoff Creamed Spinach

2 cups half-and-half
1 cup milk
1½ teaspoons chicken base, or 1 cube chicken bouillon
½ teaspoon Tabasco sauce
½ teaspoon ground nutmeg
¼ teaspoon granulated garlic
⅛ teaspoon celery salt
4 tablespoons (½ stick) unsalted butter
¼ cup all-purpose flour
3 (10-ounce) packages frozen chopped spinach, thawed
  and squeezed dry (2½ cups)
Salt and ground white pepper, if desired
Ground nutmeg, for garnish
Crisp, cooked, crumbled bacon, for garnish

In a medium-sized saucepan, heat the half-and-half, milk, chicken base, Tabasco, and seasonings to a simmer. Remove from the heat and keep warm.

In another medium-sized saucepan, heat the butter over medium heat. Add the flour and whisk well to combine. Cook this mixture for 2 to 3 minutes, stirring often. Slowly whisk the heated milk mixture into the butter mixture, a little at a time, whisking constantly until smooth. Bring the mixture to a simmer and cook for 5 minutes, stirring constantly, until it thickens. The sauce will be very thick.

Stir in the spinach and simmer for 5 minutes. Adjust seasonings. Serve while hot.

To serve: Place the hot creamed spinach in a bowl, sprinkled with an extra touch of ground nutmeg on top. Top each serving with 1 tablespoon of crisp, cooked, crumbled bacon, if desired.

Note: Granulated garlic is dried granular garlic, not the same as dried minced, dried chopped or garlic powder. It has the best flavor of all the dried garlic products, in our opinion. Some supermarkets carry it in the gourmet spice section, and it's available from spice shops.

Variation

To make the recipe with fresh spinach, you will need 4 10-ounce bags of trimmed, washed spinach (not baby spinach).

Working in four batches, wash one bagful of spinach at a time in a basin of cold water. Drain in a colander. Place the batch in a 6-quart pot over high heat, cover and steam. While the spinach is steaming, repeat the process for the other three bags, putting each on top of the spinach in the pot (it will shrink down considerably). Cover and steam until the spinach is wilted and cooked. Drain in a large colander. Press down on the spinach with a spatula to extract as much water as possible. Transfer the spinach to a cutting board and chop finely.

Line the colander with a lint-free, clean kitchen towel. Put in the chopped spinach, bring up the ends of the towel and, as soon as it's cool enough to handle, twist the towel to form a sack and squeeze dry. You should have 2½ cups of cooked, chopped, squeezed spinach.

Stir the spinach into the cream mixture and simmer for 5 minutes, stirring to mix. Adjust the seasonings. Serve hot.

ANDERSONVILLE COFFEE CAKE

It's hard to believe that at one time there were more Swedes in Chicago than in any city outside Stockholm, with most of them settled in the North Side neighborhood of Andersonville. At the heart of this charming village within the city, still home to one of the most concentrated communities of Swedish culture in the United States, you'll find the Swedish Bakery. Since it opened in the late 1920s, this old-world Scandinavian bakery has been baking up delectable pastries made with cardamom, saffron, anise, fennel, orange peel and almond paste—the spices of Sweden. The store's most popular item is its Andersonville Coffee Cake, a wreath-shaped coffee cake with a black cardamom spiked dough and a sweet almond and cinnamon filling. It's a taste of Sweden via Chicago and serves as the perfect accompaniment to a hot cup of coffee on a chilly Chicago day.

The Swedish Bakery has switched hands several times since it was first opened in the late 1920s by a certain Johnson family. Today, it's owned by Marlies Stanton, a pastry chef by trade who immigrated to Chicago from Germany in 1952. Stanton, who honed her craft while working her way up in the pastry department at the Edgewater Beach Hotel, still works long hours at the bakery, together with her children. "Mom works circles around us," laughs Marlies's daughter, Kathleen Stanton-Cromwell.

As soon as you enter the bakery, you'll be struck by the warm scents of Sweden. Look for the Swedish flags, which indicate traditionally Swedish treats, and stock up on marzariners, little iced almond tarts;

Andersonville Coffee Cake, the perfect accompaniment to a hot cup of coffee, fresh from the Swedish Bakery. *Chelsea Gibson.*

ginger pepparkaka cookies; and brusselkakas, drommars, bondkakas and havrekakas—all Swedish-style butter cookies. Arrive in the morning, when Andersonville Coffee Cakes are still warm from the oven, and buy three: one to accompany your tea in the afternoon, one for breakfast the next day and one to gift to a friend who will love you forever.

Andersonville Coffee Cake

Dough

12 tablespoons butter

2 cups milk

1 (2-ounce) yeast cake

¾ cup sugar

1 teaspoon ground black cardamom

6 cups flour

Filling

6 tablespoons butter or margarine, softened

½ cup sugar

½ tablespoon cinnamon

½ cup almonds, ground or chopped

Topping

1 egg, beaten

½ cup pearl sugar

½ cup chopped almonds

Melt butter in saucepan. Add milk and remove from heat. Crumble yeast into a large mixing bowl. In a small bowl, mix together sugar and cardamom. Add sugar cardamom mixture to the yeast and add milk mixture. Stir in the flour a little at a time and work dough until smooth and shiny. Cover and let rise for 10 minutes.

To make the filling, combine butter, sugar, cinnamon and nuts.

Preheat the oven to 400° Fahrenheit. Turn dough out onto a board and knead well. Divide into 4 parts. Roll each piece into a 14- by 8-inch rectangle. Spread with filling. Roll up from the long side and place on a baking sheet. Clip each at 1-inch intervals with scissors held perpendicular to the top. Pull each cut out to the sides, alternately, to make a pattern exposing the filling. Brush with beaten egg and sprinkle with pearl sugar and chopped almonds.

Bake for 15 to 20 minutes. Do not overbrown.

Recipe courtesy of Swedish Bakery

MARGIE'S ATOMIC SUNDAE

Nothing says summer quite like an Atomic Sundae from Margie's Candies, with its three jumbo scoops of house-made ice cream, swirls of whipped cream, rich sprinkling of nuts, wafer cookie and, of course, a cherry on top. The hot fudge arrives in a silver sauce boat so you can swirl it on as you like and scrape off every last sweet bit with a spoon.

Peter George Poulos first opened his ice cream parlor on the corner of Milwaukee and Armitage Streets in 1921. It didn't officially become Margie's Candies until 1933, when George named it after Margie Michaels, his pretty young wife.

Anyone who's anyone in the city of Chicago dipped a spoon into a Margie's sundae. The Oak Theatre (1910–75), a vaudeville and movie house once located across the street, guaranteed a post-show flow of small- and big-time celebrities. Al Capone stepped in on a regular basis to enjoy his favorite: the Black Walnut Sundae.

The sundaes are the stars of the menu at Margie's. Served in giant white clamshell-shaped dishes, all sundaes come with a silver pitcher filled with delectable, warm, house-made caramel or hot fudge sauce. The Turtle Split (three scoops of French vanilla and bananas topped with whipped cream and kettle-fresh caramel and fudge sauce) is always a classic, while Margie's Melody (a whimsical sundae combination of ice cream flavors topped with marshmallow sauce, whipped cream, nuts and, of course, a cherry) has been a Margie's favorite since the 1940s. Only the most daring patrons have what it takes to conquer the World's Largest Sundae: a half gallon of ice cream

Margie's Atomic Sundae, the Beatles' pick for a post-show splurge. *Chelsea Gibson.*

Margie's Candies: placing cherries atop sundaes and life since 1921. *Paul Beaty.*

with flavors reminiscent of the tropics. It's even sweeter if you share the happiness that is a Margie's sundae—so remember to ask for two spoons. Countless couples have fallen in love in this charming, old-school ice cream parlor.

On August 20, 1965, the Beatles played at Comisky Park. Over fifty thousand fans paid $5.50 to see the Fab Four in action. After the show, George, John, Paul and Ringo sneaked over to Margie's with five lucky girls. They ordered several Atomic Sundaes before calling it a night and heading back to the Sahara Inn in Schiller Park, bellies filled to the brim with ice cream. Margie's still keeps Beatles memorabilia in its glass display case as a reminder of that unforgettable night.

To make your own Atomic Sundae, choose three of your favorite ice cream flavors and top with Margie's inspired hot fudge sauce, a generous swirl of whipped cream, a sprinkle of chopped peanuts and a maraschino cherry.

Margie's Inspired Hot Fudge Sundae Sauce

4 tablespoons (½ stick) butter
3 squares unsweetened baking chocolate
½ cup heavy cream
1 cup granulated sugar
1 teaspoon pure vanilla extract
Pinch of salt

Microwave the butter, chocolate and cream uncovered, on high, for 1 minute. Stir. Microwave another minute. Repeat until butter and chocolate are melted.

Stir in the sugar and microwave 1 minute, uncovered. Remove and stir well with a wire whisk. Microwave another 30 seconds, then stir again. Repeat until the sugar has melted well with the butter and chocolate.

Whisk in the vanilla extract and salt. Serve warm in a silver sauce boat.

FANNIE MAY PIXIES

If your life is anything like a box of Fannie May chocolates, it's sure to be sweet. Ever since the first Fannie May store opened at the corner of Madison and LaSalle Streets in 1920, Fannie May has been a beloved Chicago favorite best known for fresh, delicious chocolates and candy confections. Even during World War II, when top-notch ingredients were scarce, Fannie May refused to substitute cheaper ingredients and chose to stick to its classic recipes, closing shop early when it ran out of quality, handcrafted chocolates.

Former journalist turned real estate magnate turned chocolatier/ horse racer H. Teller Archibald and his wife, Mildred, chose the name Fannie May for its old-fashioned ring. Their focus was on hand-dipped, house-made chocolates at a time when candy was moving into mass production. By 1930, thirty-five Fannie May shops dotted the city of Chicago, and Archibald's lucky horses raced in the East Coast stakes with candy-inspired names, including Candy Prince and Candy Maid. When the Archibalds divorced in 1929, Mildred won $1 million in alimony, attesting to Fannie May's early success.

Fannie May Pixies—fresh, crunchy pecans smothered in buttery caramel and drenched in silky-smooth chocolate—were first created just after World War II. Since then, Valentine's Day and Mother's Day call for a box of freshly dipped Pixies tied with a bow. During the holidays, the creamy, crunchy confection takes on a more festive look with delicately drizzled red and green stripes.

Ever since Fannie May opened its first store at the corner of Madison and LaSalle Streets in Chicago in 1920, it has been a go-to spot for fresh, delicious chocolates and candy confections. Storefront in the Loop. *Fannie May.*

Pixie-Inspired Chocolate Pecan Caramel Candies

1 cup pecan halves
1 cup unwrapped Fannie May caramel squares
1 cup milk chocolate chips
1 cup semisweet chocolate chips

Preheat oven to 300° Fahrenheit.

Spread the pecans on a cookie baking sheet lined with parchment paper. Toast for 10 minutes, until golden brown. Set aside the toasted pecans and chill the baking sheet.

Place 3 pecan halves in a Y shape on the foil with 1 caramel candy at the center of each. Bake just until caramel is melted, about 10 minutes.

Heat the chocolate chips in a double boiler until melted. Spread chocolate over candies. Allow candies to firm up in the fridge for about 30 minutes before serving.

MAURICE LENELL PINWHEELS

At trip to Maurice Lenell's former cookie factory on Harlem Avenue in Norridge was once a childhood rite of passage. To see the cookies tumble down the conveyor belt, fresh from the oven, was delightful; to be able to eat as many broken cookies as you wanted was nothing short of heavenly. While the company was known for its many cookie types, including chocolate chip, English toffee and jelly stars, Maurice Lenell's pinwheels, with their chocolate and vanilla swirls and pink sugared edges, were the stars.

Like many other iconic Chicago treats, Maurice Lenell cookies are the product of the hard-won American dream come true. Brothers Hans and Gunnar Lenell and their friend Aagard Billing emigrated from Sweden to Chicago, where they opened a bakery that cranked out all the Swedish treats that the growing Swedish population so missed from the old country. More than anything, however, customers adored their buttery cookies. The trio capitalized on their reputation for baking the best cookies this side of Sweden and opened Lenell's Cookies, which later morphed into Maurice Lenell's Cooky Company.

In 2008, the company went bankrupt, and Maurice Lenell's pinwheels ceased rolling down the assembly line, causing many broken hearts. Here's the recipe that will bring their delightful swirls back to life once again.

Icebox Pinwheel Cookies

3 cups all-purpose flour
½ teaspoon baking powder
½ teaspoon salt
1 cup unsalted butter
1⅓ cups sugar
2 eggs
2 teaspoons vanilla extract
2 ounces unsweetened chocolate, melted

Sift the flour, baking powder and salt together and set aside.

In a mixer with a paddle attachment, cream the butter well, then add the sugar and continue creaming until light and fluffy. Add the eggs 1 at a time and then the vanilla.

On the low setting, add the dry ingredients and mix just until combined. Divide the dough in half and return half the dough to the mixer. Add the warm melted chocolate and mix to combine. Shape both pieces of dough into 4- by 4-inch squares. Wrap them in plastic wrap and chill for 30 minutes.

Cut each square into 4 strips, then place them on a sheet pan and keep chilled while you roll out the dough. Between pieces of parchment paper, roll out a piece of chocolate dough into a 6- by 7-inch rectangle (have a ruler nearby). Roll a piece of vanilla dough out into a 6- by 6-inch square. Peel off the top pieces of parchment from both doughs and flip the vanilla dough onto the chocolate, allowing for a ½-inch border of chocolate dough around the top and bottom. Press the 2 doughs together lightly with a cake pan or other flat pan. Peel off the top piece of parchment and fold the ½-inch of overhanging chocolate dough up and over the vanilla dough. Use the parchment to roll up the dough into a tight pinwheel. Wrap in plastic wrap and chill 4 to 5 hours (roll the dough a couple times in the first hour so it doesn't develop a flat side). Repeat with the remaining pieces of dough.

Preheat the oven to 350° Fahrenheit. Butter a sheet pan. Unwrap the roll and cut into ¼-inch slices. Place them 1½ inches apart on the sheet pan and bake for 9 to 11 minutes.

Recipe slightly adapted from Gale Gand by Molly Smith of ModernPrairie.com

FLAMING SAGANAKI

Chicago's Parthenon Restaurant is Greektown's oldest restaurant and the honored birthplace of flambéed saganaki, an iconic Greek American favorite. Dining in the restaurant today, you're bound to hear many merry exclamations of "Opa!"—a common Greek celebratory expression that originally meant "Oops!"—as waiters set a square of traditional Greek cheese drenched in brandy alight, thus flambéing it tableside. With a squeeze of lemon juice, the flames die out, and the sizzling, salty-sweet saganaki is ready to be enjoyed, alone or with a hunk of crusty, house-made bread.

The story of Greek American brothers Chris and Bill Liakouras involves no lucky "Opa"-style moments but rather a lifetime of hard work and dedication to their family business. The duo worked as waiters for eight years after immigrating to America, saving up to open their American dream—the Parthenon Restaurant—in 1968. The Parthenon features over 140 dishes on its menu of Greek delights, but no meal is complete without flaming saganaki.

Legend has it that a few days after the restaurant opened, a group of Greek women hanging out at the restaurant's bar suggested flambéing a plate of cheese saganaki with a little brandy for show.

Chicago-style Flaming Saganaki calls for graviera, halloumi, kasseri, kefalograviera, kefalotyri or sheep's milk feta cheese. The Parthenon uses kasseri. Dust the cheese with flour and then heat on a butter-laden skillet until golden brown on both sides. Pour in a jigger of

Above: Just say, "OPA!" *Chelsea Gibson.*

Left: Flambéed saganaki, an iconic Greek American favorite invented in Chicago. Flaming Saganaki at Greek Islands. *Greek Islands.*

The Parthenon features over 140 dishes on its menu of Greek delights, but no meal is complete without saganaki flambé. *Chelsea Gibson.*

brandy, light it with a long match and shout "Opa!" as loudly as your lungs will let you. Douse the flames with the squeeze of a lemon and serve with a loaf of the crustiest Greek bread you can find. If you're in Chicago, head to Pan Hellenic Bakery (322 South Halsted Street) for warm-from-the-oven bread.

The Liakouras brothers initially went even further and offered a free saganaki to every diner, drawing in customers with their dazzling new dish. The restaurant, which today is run by Chris Liakouras's daughter, claims on its website: "Before saganaki was flambéed here, it was merely fried cheese."

Flaming Saganaki

2½-inch-thick slices of kasseri cheese
Flour for dusting
2 tablespoons butter
½ shot glass of brandy
1 lemon, cut into wedges

Dust the cheese lightly with flour. Add the butter in a small skillet and heat until melted. Dredge the cheese in flour, then heat in the skillet until golden brown on both sides.

Remove skillet from stove, pour 1 jigger of warmed brandy over the cheese, light with a long matchstick and shout, "Opa!" Douse the flame with a lemon wedge.

Serve immediately with a crusty loaf of bread.

BOOKBINDER RED SNAPPER SOUP

For more than ninety years, Chicago's Drake Hotel has been welcoming visitors from its perch at the start of the Magnificent Mile. The hotel's acclaimed Cape Cod Room, opened in 1933, is still one of the best spots in the city to enjoy a fresh Atlantic or Pacific catch. The restaurant's décor hasn't changed much since opening day—its nautical, faded elegance is still so charming; its seafood still sublime.

"Most of the classic recipes haven't changed since the Cape Cod Room first opened," explains senior sous chef Hillary York. "It's one of the main reasons I love working here—all of the traditions." The Cape Cod Room welcomed its first diners aboard on December 6, 1933, the day after the Twenty-First Amendment was ratified, bringing an end to Prohibition. Opening day lines were so long with alcohol-thirsty patrons that the bartenders resorted to pouring forty-cent shots of whiskey to keep everyone happy and tipsy.

Bookbinder Soup is one of the restaurant's specialties. The original recipe, created in 1893 by Samuel Bookbinder of the Old Original Bookbinder's restaurant in Philadelphia, was gifted to the Drake to celebrate its inauguration. Over the years, the recipe for this savory, tomato-based vegetable soup was adapted by the Cape Cod Room. The biggest change occurred when snapping turtle was replaced with red snapper, though no one quite remembers when that change was made. The price of the soup has changed as well: on the original menu, a cup cost a whopping thirty-five cents and a bowl, fifty cents. The soup is still served with a small cruet of dry sherry, as per tradition.

The acclaimed Cape Cod Room, opened in 1933, is still one of the best spots in the city to enjoy a fresh Atlantic or Pacific catch. Bookbinder Soup is one of the restaurant's most sought-after specialties. *Chelsea Gibson.*

For a truly unique meal, start your Cape Cod Room experience with freshly shucked oysters and a glass of straight gin at the bar. See if you can spot the initials of Joe DiMaggio and Marilyn Monroe, carved into the northern end of the wooden bar while they were on a whirlwind date at the Cape Cod Room in 1954, the same year they were married and divorced. The bartender keeps a flashlight to spotlight it in case you can't.

Bookbinder Red Snapper Soup

Preparation, Part 1

1 carrot, chopped
1 small stalk of celery, chopped
1 clove fresh garlic, crushed
½ ounce clarified butter
2 quarts vegetable stock
1 bay leaf
8 crushed white peppercorns
Pinch of thyme
Pinch of sage
Pinch of oregano
½ cup tomato paste
Salt to taste

In a stock pot, sauté the carrot, celery and garlic in the butter. Add the vegetable stock, spices and tomato paste and simmer for 20 minutes. Salt to taste. Strain and set aside.

Preparation, Part 2

½ small onion, diced
1 small stalk of celery, chopped
½ ounce clarified butter
10 ounces poached red snapper, diced
3 tablespoons California sherry

Sauté the onion and celery until tender in butter. Add the red snapper and sherry. Sauté the red snapper until opaque throughout, about 2 to 3 minutes on each side. Add to the broth. Serve with a cruet of fine dry sherry on the side.

Recipe courtesy of the Drake Hotel

MRS. HERRING'S CHICKEN POT PIE

Marshall Field was a Chicago entrepreneur, innovator and founder of his eponymous department store. Though it was acquired by Macy's, Inc. in 2005, most Chicagoans have refused to acknowledge the name change, sticking with the shortened version, Fields. Surely Marshall Field, the man behind the name, would have been proud to see his namesake store still so well regarded 137 years after Chicago business mogul Potter Palmer convinced him and his partner, Levi Leiter, to lease a new, six-story edifice at the northeast corner of State and Washington Streets.

Marshall Field's introduced so many elements to the shopping experience: revolving credit, the bridal registry, in-store escalators, overseas buying offices, personal shoppers and, above all, superior customer service. Marshall Field's was also the first department store ever to introduce the concept of in-store dining with the Walnut Room, its seventh-floor, full-service restaurant.

In the nineteenth century, it was considered in poor taste for a lady to dine alone. When a kindly Marshall Field's clerk, Mrs. Herring, shared her lunch with a tired shopper, a light bulb went off. An observant Marshall Field, whose famous slogan was "Give the lady what she wants," recognized the need to better accommodate his female customers and, in turn, increase sales. The South Tea Room was opened in the 1880s; in 1907, it became known officially as the Walnut Room. Mrs. Herring's Chicken Pot Pie, a perennial favorite, remains on the menu to this day as a tribute to the kindly woman who sparked the in-store tearoom concept.

During the holiday season, the Walnut Room is especially reminiscent of Christmases of days gone by in Chicago, and a visit has become a holiday tradition for generations of Chicagoans. At the center of the elegant dining room stands the forty-five-foot-tall Great Tree, decked out in over fifteen thousand lights and more than 1,200 themed ornaments, always a grand symbol of the holidays. It takes two days to construct and decorate the Great Tree. The tree hangs from the ceiling because it sits atop the Tiffany Dome, a city treasure, so it's decorated from top to bottom—the star is the first decoration to adorn the tree each year. Long ago, the Great Tree was real and required an on-site team of firemen to ensure that it didn't catch fire!

Mrs. Herring's Chicken Pot Pie

This recipe is adapted from the original, published in the now out-of-print Marshall Field's Cookbook. *Mrs. Herring's Chicken Pot Pie is a winter favorite guaranteed to warm your belly and your soul on a cold evening.*

6 tablespoons unsalted butter
1 large onion, diced
3 carrots, thinly sliced
3 celery stalks, sliced
½ cup all-purpose flour
1½ cups milk
2½ cups chicken broth
3 cups cooked chicken, shredded
1 teaspoon chopped fresh thyme leaves
¼ cup dry sherry
¾ cup frozen green peas, thawed
2 tablespoons minced fresh parsley
2 teaspoons salt
½ teaspoon freshly ground black pepper
1 sheet frozen puff pastry dough, thawed
1 egg, whisked with 1 tablespoon water

Preheat the oven to 400° Fahrenheit. Place a large saucepan over medium heat and add the butter. When the butter is melted, add the onion, carrots, and celery and cook, stirring occasionally, for 10 minutes, until the onion is soft and translucent. Add the flour and cook, stirring, for 1 minute. Slowly whisk in the milk and chicken broth. Decrease the heat to low and simmer, stirring often, for 10 minutes. Add the chicken, thyme, sherry, peas, parsley, salt and pepper and stir well. Divide the warm filling among six 10- or 12-ounce potpie tins or individual ramekins.

Cut the puff pastry dough into 6 rounds and lay a round over each pot pie filling. Tuck the overhanging dough back under itself and flute the edges with a fork. Cut a 1-inch slit in the top of each pie. Brush the tops of the pies with the egg wash.

Line a baking sheet with aluminum foil or parchment paper. Place the pies on the baking sheet and bake for 25 minutes, until the pastry is golden and the filling is bubbling. Serve hot.

TAYLOR STREET
ITALIAN LEMONADE

On hot summer nights, you're bound to find plenty of people milling about Chicago's Little Italy, dipping into a cool Italian ice. The line in front of Mario's Italian Lemonade will be running out onto the street, where curbside seating is available for Italian ice lovers too tired to stand and eat.

When Mario DiPaolo was a little boy in the mid-1950s, he was so rambunctious that his parents decided to put his energy to work. Mario's dad parked a shaved ice maker in front of their little storefront on Taylor Street, and Mario happily hand-cranked his way to fame. Though Mario's no longer uses the hand-crank method, and though a cup of Mario's old-fashioned lemonade ice no longer costs two cents, when Mario's Lemonade reopens every year in May, summertime in Chicago can officially commence.

Mario's original stand-alone shaved ice maker has been replaced by a wooden lemonade stand that's small in stature but big in Italian pride, thanks to its green, white and red paint job. Mario's is located on Taylor Street, the heart of Chicago's Little Italy, a vibrant hub of Italian American culture anchored by the Shrine of Our Lady of Pompeii.

Mario's Italian lemonade is an Americanized take on the traditional Italian granita, a slushy, shaved ice flavored with fruity syrups. These are no factory-made syrups either—they're the real deal, made on-site from fresh fruits, as evidenced in the minuscule rinds of lemon found in every icy concoction. Originally, Mario only offered one flavor—lemon—and

Though Mario's no longer uses the hand-crank method, and though a cup of Mario's old-fashioned lemonade ice no longer costs two cents, when Mario's Lemonade reopens every year in May, summertime in Chicago can officially commence. *Paul Beaty.*

to this day, lemon is the most popular of the bunch, as well as the base of all other flavors, which range across the fruit rainbow. Even the subtly rich chocolate flavor has a lemon base, adding an unbeatable tang to the sweetness of the experience. You'll find more than a dozen rotating flavors on the handwritten menu board to choose from, but the fan favorites remain peach and, of course, lemon. Avoid a terrible case of brain freeze by slurping the deliciousness with a spoon.

Taylor Street Italian Lemonade

3 cups water
1 cup sugar
1 cup fresh lemon juice (about 7 lemons)
1 tablespoon grated lemon rind

Combine 1 cup of the water with the sugar in a saucepan and simmer over medium heat, stirring constantly, until the sugar is completely dissolved. Stir in the remaining water and let cool to room temperature. Stir in the lemon juice and lemon peel.

Pour the mixture into a chilled 10- by 12-inch metal baking pan. After 1 hour, remove from freezer and scrape the ice with a fork, making sure to mix the outer ice crystals with the still-unfrozen center. Return to the freezer.

After 2 hours, scoop the ice into cups. If the ice is frozen solid and difficult to scoop, let it sit out for 5 minutes and then blend in a food processor until slushy.

STUFFED MELROSE PEPPERS

L egend has it that a family emigrating from Italy to the United States carried with them the cherished seeds of the tender, supersweet peppers that so reminded them of home. Once planted in the garden of their new home in Melrose Park, Illinois—a near-western suburb of Chicago—the peppers, like the many Italians who immigrated to the Chicago area, thrived. A new Italian pepper variety was born, named after its new suburban home: the Melrose pepper.

The four-inch, thick-skinned peppers are rich, flavorful and mild. They're best served stuffed with Italian spices, sausages and cheeses that complement their sweetness. You'll find them only in Chicagoland in the summertime, at farmer's markets or at area Italian grocers. If you have a green thumb, you can find Melrose pepper seeds online and grow your own.

Legend has it that a family emigrating from Italy to the United States carried with them the cherished seeds of the tender, super sweet peppers used to make Stuffed Melrose Peppers. *Marie Renello from ProudItalianCook.com.*

Stuffed Melrose Peppers. *Marie Renello from ProudItalianCook.com.*

Stuffed Melrose Peppers

12 Melrose peppers
1 cup ricotta cheese
1 cup freshly grated parmesan cheese
3 cloves minced garlic
2 teaspoons crushed red pepper flakes
3 tablespoons fresh basil, chopped
3 tablespoons fresh parsley, chopped
2 pounds Italian sausage
Olive oil
3 cups marinara sauce

Cut the tops off the peppers and remove the seeds. Mix together the ricotta and parmesan cheese. Add garlic and spices. Place the mixture in a Ziploc bag and cut a tip off for easy pepper stuffing.

Stuff the peppers with Italian sausage and cheese mixture. Sauté the stuffed peppers in olive oil in a large frying pan until the peppers are tender and the sausage partially cooked. Add the marinara, cover and cook for 20 more minutes.

Serve with a crusty loaf of Italian bread.

Recipe courtesy of Marie Renello of prouditaliancook.com

ITALIAN BEEF SANDWICH

Few things in life beat biting into a dense Italian roll packed with thin slices of seasoned roast beef, dripping with savory jus and topped off with Chicago-style giardiniera or sautéed green Italian sweet peppers. The Italian beef sandwich is not just a Chicago-born and bred favorite; it's an icon. Born out of the Great Depression, the Italian beef sandwich calls for tougher and hence cheaper cuts of meat. Cooked for several hours, then sliced super thin and served on a big roll drenched in the beef's spiced cooking juices, this is a sandwich that stretches the meaty flavor while also filling up your belly. Legend states that the sandwich was invented by Italian immigrants working for the Union Stockyards: they transformed the tougher rump cut into what is now known as a de facto Chicago delicacy.

In 1925, Italian immigrant Pasquale Scala saw his American dream come true when he began supplying Italian sausage and beef—thinly sliced so it went further among guests—to weddings and banquets. Al Ferrari and his sister and brother-in-law, Frances and Chris Pacelli Sr., claim to have developed the idea and recipe for the original Italian beef sandwich, transforming Scala's ultra-thinly sliced beef into a sandwich that was thick on flavor. Al's Beef was one of the first stands to serve up the sandwiches, beginning in 1938, followed by Mr. Beef, Buona Beef and Carm's Beef—all of which are related via family connections, making the Italian Beef Sandwich truly a product of the Italian American dream, built on the foundation that is *la famiglia*.

If you want to eat an Italian beef in Chicago, you need to know the lingo. Wet or dipped means that the roll has been quickly immersed in its jus.

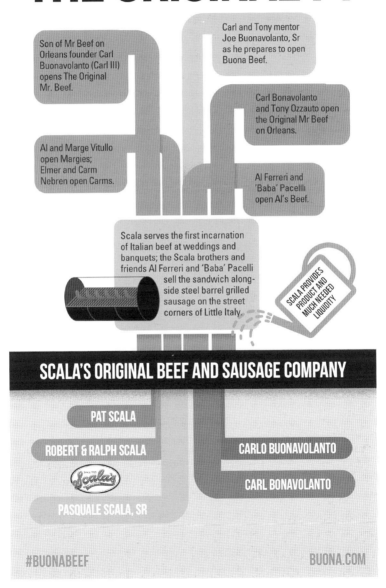

CHICAGO'S ITALIAN BEEF
THE ORIGINAL 14

Son of Mr Beef on Orleans founder Carl Buonavolanto (Carl III) opens The Original Mr. Beef.

Carl and Tony mentor Joe Buonavolanto, Sr as he prepares to open Buona Beef.

Carl Bonavolanto and Tony Ozzauto open the Original Mr Beef on Orleans.

Al and Marge Vitullo open Margies; Elmer and Carm Nebren open Carms.

Al Ferreri and 'Baba' Pacelli open Al's Beef.

Scala serves the first incarnation of Italian beef at weddings and banquets; the Scala brothers and friends Al Ferreri and 'Baba' Pacelli sell the sandwich alongside steel barrel grilled sausage on the street corners of Little Italy.

SCALA PROVIDES PRODUCT AND MUCH NEEDED LIQUIDITY

SCALA'S ORIGINAL BEEF AND SAUSAGE COMPANY

PAT SCALA

ROBERT & RALPH SCALA

CARLO BUONAVOLANTO

CARL BONAVOLANTO

PASQUALE SCALA, SR

#BUONABEEF

BUONA.COM

"The Genealogy of the Italian Beef Sandwich." *Graphic courtesy of Buona Beef.*

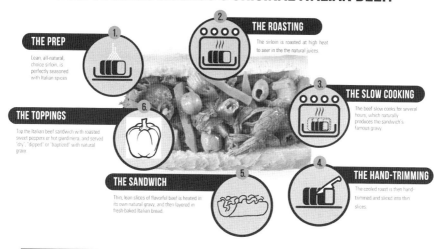

BEEFOGRAPHY
HOW TO MAKE CHICAGO'S ORIGINAL ITALIAN BEEF.

THE PREP
Lean, all-natural, choice sirloin, is perfectly seasoned with Italian spices

2. THE ROASTING
The sirloin is roasted at high heat to sear in the the natural juices.

3. THE SLOW COOKING
The beef slow cooks for several hours, which naturally produces the sandwich's famous gravy.

THE TOPPINGS
Top the Italian beef sandwich with roasted sweet peppers or hot giardiniera, and served 'dry', 'dipped' or 'baptized' with natural gravy.

THE SANDWICH
Thin, lean slices of flavorful beef is heated in its own natural gravy, and then layered in fresh-baked Italian bread.

4. THE HAND-TRIMMING
The cooled roast is then hand-trimmed and sliced into thin slices.

*There are no shortcuts to authenticity. When it's cooked right, the roast gets smaller – about 45% smaller. Some folks reduce cooking times, pump water back into the roast to make it bigger, and add unnatural ingredients to the gravy. Our family would never dream of doing this and remain true to the original Italian beef receipe.

#BUONABEEF

BUONA.COM

Beefography Chart. *Graphic courtesy of Buona Beef.*

Juicy means it's immersed just a little bit longer. Go for soaked or baptized and your sandwich will be completely dipped and arrive dripping wet and delicious. Order your sandwich dry and it won't be soaked at all. Go for a combo and you'll find an Italian sausage nestled in the roll, too. Order a hot dipped and you'll get an extra dose of spicy giardiniera, while sweet calls for roasted green peppers. The ultimate gut-buster, however, is the triple double: double sausage, double cheese (mozzarella or provolone) and double beef, packed into a bun and ready to conquer your belly.

Finally, learn how to eat a dripping, delicious Italian beef sandwich the right way. Most Chicago Italian beef joints have long countertops so you can lean in and employ the "Italian stance." Jimmie the Beef Guy, Italian beef aficionado and owner of italianbeef.com, explains it best: Put your sandwich on the counter and stand in front of it, with your chest about twelve inches from the edge of the counter. Lean forward so your chest is at a forty-five-degree-angle to the counter. (Note: if you're wearing a tie, make sure it's tucked inside your shirt.) Pick up your sandwich, resting your elbows on the counter. Angle the sandwich at a forty-five-degree angle to the counter, with the top end toward your mouth. Imagine making a triangle: the counter is the bottom, your head and chest are one side and the sandwich is another. Eat and enjoy. For best results, keep the sandwich wrapped in the wax paper it most likely came in, unwrapping it as you go.

Italian Beef Sandwich

5 pounds rump roast

4 cups beef broth (or 4 cups water and 5 cubes beef bouillon)

2 tablespoons Worcestershire sauce

2 teaspoons ground black pepper

1 tablespoon dried oregano

1 tablespoon dried parsley

1 tablespoon dried basil

1 tablespoon garlic powder

1 tablespoon onion powder

1 tablespoon crushed red pepper

Pinch of thyme

Large Italian bread rolls

Giardiniera (see recipe on pages 14–15)

Add all of the ingredients to your trusty slow cooker and cook on low for 18 hours, turning roast every 4 to 6 hours. Shred the meat with a fork and pile it onto a roll, adding cooking juice to taste.

CRACKER JACK

Cracker Jack is one of the first treats to be born and raised in Chicago. It all started with German immigrant Frederick William Rueckheim, aka "Fritz," who sold his steam-popped popcorn coated in molasses and studded with roasted peanuts from his South Side candy shop at 113 Fourth Avenue (eventually renamed Federal Street) in Chicago, beginning in 1871. In 1873, Fritz's brother, Louis, also immigrated to Chicago from Germany to help the booming popcorn business, and in 1893, the brothers banded together to launch Cracker Jack at the World's Columbian Exposition. In 1896, Louis came up with an ingenious method that prevented the sticky popcorn from clumping together—a secret, industry formula that remains a secret and is still in use today. Later that same year, the name Cracker Jack—slang for "fantastic" at the time—was registered.

Cracker Jack was the source of yet another manufacturing innovation in 1899, when Henry Gottlieb Eckstein developed the "waxed sealed package," aka "Eckstein Triple Proof Package," extending Cracker Jack's shelf life. By the time lyricist Jack Norworth and composer Albert Von Tilzer added, "Buy me some peanuts and Cracker Jack" to their 1908 hit "Take Me Out to the Ball Game," Cracker Jack had become not just a Chicago-born snack but also an American icon.

When the company introduced its prize in every package marketing ploy in 1912, the Cracker Jack Company employed about 450 women and girls and 250 men and boys at its factory on South Peoria and Harrison Streets. Kids eagerly opened their boxes to reveal a puzzle, plastic figurine, whistle, mini magnifying lens or even a secret decoder ring. In 1914, Cracker Jack issued baseball cards, which today remain highly sought-after collector's items, some of which are worth thousands of dollars.

In 1916, Cracker Jack's mascot, a sailor named Jack and his dog, Bingo, sailed onto the boxes. Sailor Jack was inspired by Fritz's grandson, Robert Rueckheim. Sadly, Robert died of pneumonia at age eight and was buried at St. Henry's Cemetery in the West Ridge neighborhood. An image of Sailor Jack once appeared on his headstone but has since been removed.

1871 Cracker Jack

This recipe is inspired by the original formula for Cracker Jack, made with molasses.

1 cup popcorn kernels (20 cups popped)
1 cup butter
2 cups brown sugar
1 cup molasses
1 teaspoon salt
1 teaspoon vanilla
1 cup roasted peanuts
1 teaspoon baking soda

Preheat oven to 250° Fahrenheit. Pop the popcorn in an air popper. Pour into a large roasting pan or aluminum tray and set aside.

Melt the butter in a large saucepan over low heat. Stir in the sugar, molasses and salt and continue to stir until the sugar dissolves. Turn off the heat and stir in the vanilla and peanuts. Stir in the baking soda.

Pour the mixture over the popcorn and toss until evenly coated. Bake in the oven for 1 hour, tossing every 15 minutes.

THE JIBARITO

Chicago is home to one of the largest Puerto Rican communities in the United States. It has its own Paseo Boricua, the only officially recognized Puerto Rican neighborhood in the nation; its own Fiestas Puertorriqueñas, an annual celebration of all things Puerto Rico—one of the largest Latin events in the nation; and even its own Puerto Rico–inspired sandwich, the mouthwatering Jibarito.

Juan "Peter" Figueroa of Old Borinquen Restaurant on California Avenue in Chicago's Humboldt Park dreamed up this unique sandwich after reading a newspaper article about a Puerto Rican sandwich that switched out the bread for plantains, an island staple. He flattened and fried green plantains, then sandwiched thinly sliced, seasoned skirt steak; lettuce; onions; and garlic

The Jibarito was dreamed up by Chicagoan Juan "Peter" Figueroa, who named his creation the Jibarito after Jíbaro, which refers to the people who live in the agricultural heart of Puerto Rico. *Ponce Restaurant, 4212 West Fullerton Street.*

mayo between the two crispy halves. He named his creation the Jibarito, which refers to the people who live in the mountainous, agricultural heart of Puerto Rico. Indeed, Figueroa's Borinquen Restaurant boomed thanks to the Jibarito, and he was able to purchase his family farm back in the central Puerto Rican farming town Jayuya.

Other Latin American restaurants around Chicago copied Figueroa's Jibarito recipe, making it a true Chicago sandwich found across the city today. Though the original Jibarito is filled with steak, you'll find other fillings, including chicken, roast pork, ham, shrimp and even tofu.

The Jibarito

5 cups vegetable oil, for frying
2 green plantains, cut in half
½ pound skirt steak, thinly sliced
Salt to taste
½ teaspoon cayenne pepper
Pinch cumin powder
1 clove garlic, minced
3 tablespoons olive oil
Garlic mayo (see page 54)
½ red onion, sliced into half moons
Lettuce

Heat oil to about 325° Farenheit, then fry the plantains for about 1 minute. Remove the plantains from oil and place on a paper towel–lined plate. Flatten plantains between two heavy cutting boards. Return the plantains to the heated oil and fry again until golden, about 2 minutes.

Season the steak with salt, cayenne, cumin powder and minced garlic. Heat the olive oil in a frying pan over medium heat. Add the steak to the pan and cook a couple minutes on each side or as preferred.

Spread garlic mayo on each side of the fried plantains, then fill your Jibarito with steak, sliced red onion and lettuce.

Garlic Mayo
½ cup mayonnaise
1 clove garlic, minced
Salt and pepper, to taste

CHICAGO-STYLE HOT DOG

Born on the pushcarts of Maxwell Street during the Great Depression, the Chicago-Style Hot Dog offered both a belly-filling meal for a mere nickel and the opportunity for new immigrants to build a small business empire.

Nestle an all-beef frankfurter—boiled, steamed or charred—in a steamed poppy seed bun, squirt on some yellow mustard and then "drag it through the garden" by adding chopped white onions, sweet pickle relish, a dill pickle spear, tomato wedges, sport peppers and a dash of celery salt for a final zing. Don't even think about adding ketchup.

The hot dog itself was an import to Chicago via Frankfurt via Vienna. Slender pork sausages, aka frankfurters, the predecessors to today's hotdog, were produced as early as the thirteenth century in Frankfurt. In the early 1800s, Vienna-based butcher Johann Georg Lahner, who apprenticed in the frankfurter capital of Frankfurt, added beef to the mixture and fittingly called it a "wiener-frankfurter."

As with so many other iconic Chicago foods, the 1893 World's Columbian Exposition played a role in the hot dog's entrance into the American palate. Austrian-Hungarian immigrants Emil Reichel and Sam Ladany sold their Vienna Beef hot dogs at the exposition, making hot dogs one of the first fair foods to exist, while also making it possible for the duo to open up their first Vienna Beef Hot Dogs storefront on Chicago's Near West Side at 417 South Halsted Avenue. Not long after, wieners wrapped in buns became a hit at baseball parks, too, settling themselves into both fair and sporting event menus. By 1908, Vienna Beef hot dogs were delivered across Chicago

Born in the street carts of Maxwell Street during the Great Depression, the Chicago-Style Hot Dog offered both a belly-filling meal for a nickel and the opportunity for new immigrants to build a fledgling first business. *Chelsea Gibson.*

Austrian-Hungarian immigrants Emil Reichel and Sam Ladany found success selling their Vienna Beef Hot Dogs at the 1893 World's Fair. With their hard-earned money, they opened up their first Vienna Beef Hot Dogs storefront on Chicago's Near West Side at 417 South Halsted Avenue. Vienna Beef smokehouse in 1935. *Image courtesy of Vienna Beef.*

By 1908, Vienna Beef hot dogs were delivered across Chicago via horse-drawn carriage. *Image courtesy of Vienna Beef.*

via horse-drawn carriage; in 1928, they shifted to a motorized delivery fleet. The Great Depression sent hot dogs soaring; for one nickel, you could count on a satiating, grab-and-go meal in a bun.

The Chicago-style tradition of "dragging the hot dog through the garden" was likely born during this difficult era, with garden-grown tomatoes, onions, cucumbers and peppers adding an extra boost of vitamins to make the hot dog a complete meal. The Chicago-Style Hot Dog is truly a treasure of our city of immigrants: Jewish bakers produced the poppy seed bun, and Italian gardeners likely supplied the sport peppers and tomatoes. Celery was introduced to the area by Dutch farmers from Michigan and then grown in Lincoln Square, where farmers, mostly of German and English descent, drove their produce in wagons down Little Fort Road, today's Lincoln Avenue, to the markets in Chicago; indeed, the Lincoln Square area once declared itself the celery capital of the world. Meanwhile, the Budlong brothers opened a pickle factory in 1836, employing Polish workers from Chicago on a seasonal basis. From carts scattered throughout the city, both newly arrived and established Chicagoans realized their small piece of the American dream by starting fledgling businesses via their hot dog carts.

In 1928, Vienna Beef shifted to a motorized delivery fleet. *Image courtesy of Vienna Beef.*

Chicago-Style Hot Dog

1 all-beef hot dog
1 poppy seed hot dog bun
Yellow mustard
Sweet green pickle relish
Chopped onionv
Tomato wedges
Dill pickle spear
Sport peppers
Dash celery salt

Bring a pot of water to a boil. Reduce heat to low, place hot dog in water and cook for 5 minutes. Place a steamer basket into the pot and steam the hot dog bun until warm.

Snuggle the hot dog in the steamed bun. Add a stripe of yellow mustard to the hot dog, then "drag it through the garden" by adding the other condiments, with a dash of celery salt for the final touch.

Warning: Do not add ketchup.

CHICKEN VESUVIO

Chicken Vesuvio is a classic Italian American dish, featuring sautéed chicken on the bone dressed with plenty of garlic, oregano, white wine and olive oil, then baked with potato wedges until golden and crispy. Legend has it that Chicken Vesuvio made its debut at Chicago's Vesuvio Restaurant in the 1930s. John Drury cites the Vesuvio in his 1931 guide, *Dining in Chicago*:

> *This Italian Restaurant…occupies one of the most cosmopolitan sites in town. It lies between the Michigan Avenue bridgehead plaza and the grand sweeping plaza at Wacker Drive and North Wabash Avenue, with the waters and the steamers of Chicago at its feet. The decorations by the Italian artist, Gallano, are Pompeian, in black, red and gold. D. Price, a native of Torino, one of the proprietors, numbers among his friends Gallli-Curci, Rosa Raisa, Tito Schipa, and other operatic notables; Rossi, the other proprietor, was formerly with the Drake and Blackstone Hotels and knows what Italian cooking is all about. Hence the reason why many bigwigs dine here frequently—Jack Dempsey and his wife, Estelle Taylor; Jackie Coogan, the kid movie actor; Edith Rockefeller McCormick, Chicago's social queen, and Count Charles de Fontnouvelle, the French consul. Business men's luncheons at 65 cents and table d'hôte dinners at $1.25 and $1.50. There are a lot of Italian specialties served here—and appetizingly too.*

Though it's best known as Chicago oldest steakhouse, Gene & Georgetti has been serving Chicken Vesuvio on its menu since the 1940s, when Chef

Legend has it that Chicken Vesuvio made its debut at the Vesuvio Restaurant in the 1930s. Gene & Georgetti's Classic Chicken Vesuvio. *Chelsea Gibson.*

Gene & Georgetti's Classic Chicken Vesuvio. *Chelsea Gibson.*

Frank Merletti created his own interpretation of the dish. Hidden in the shadow of the El's Brown line, in a classic 1870s wood-frame house, Gene & Georgetti was the realization of the American dream for partners Gene Michelotti and Alfredo "Georgetti" Federighi. While working as a bartender, Michelotti encountered his future business partner, Federighi, who was working as a chef. In 1941, Gene & Georgetti opened its doors, with Alfredo manning the kitchen and Gene working the front and holding down the bar. The restaurant is still in family hands: Gene's daughter Marion and her husband, Tony Durpetti, work hard to keep the restaurant in the family while also treating their staff and customers like family. Step up to the second floor, where you'll find a mural depicting the neighborhood as it was when the steakhouse opened, a primarily Italian American area anchored by the Church of the Assumption (323 West Illinois Street).

Chicken Vesuvio

1 large fryer (3½ to 4 pounds), cut into 8 pieces
3 medium Idaho potatoes, about 1¼ pounds total
⅓ cup olive oil
4 large cloves garlic, minced
2 teaspoons dried oregano
3 tablespoons fresh parsley, minced
⅓ cup dry white wine (chablis or Italian chardonnay)

Preheat oven to 425° Fahrenheit. Keep the skin on the chicken. Wash and pat dry with paper towels. Peel the potatoes and then cut each half into 4 long quarters. Pat dry.

Add olive oil to a large, shallow roasting pan and put over medium/high heat. When oil is hot, arrange chicken and potatoes, rounded side down, in a single layer in pan. Cook 5 minutes, carefully shaking pan often to prevent sticking. Do not turn.

Transfer chicken and potatoes to oven. Bake for 20 minutes. Use a spatula to turn chicken and potatoes and bake until both are golden and crispy and juice runs clear rather than pink when thigh is pierced with a knife. Bake about 10 minutes more.

Working quickly, season chicken and potatoes with salt and pepper. Sprinkle with garlic, oregano and parsley and toss gently to mix. Add wine and gently shake pan to mix. Transfer chicken, potatoes and pan juices to a warm platter. Serve immediately.

Recipe courtesy of Gene & Georgetti

CHICAGO-STYLE HOT TAMALES

Chicago-Style Hot Tamales offer a unique take on the traditional tamale. Smooth, machine-extruded cornmeal is filled with mildly spiced and seasoned ground beef, wrapped in parchment paper and cooked in a steamer. They truly are hot tamales. Served on the streets of Chicago since at least the late 1800s, their origin is a mystery, though there are a few clues that seem to indicate they came to Chicago via Mississippi, not Mexico, as many might assume.

In 1909, Chicago-born ragtime pianist Herbert Ingraham published "The Hot Tamale Man," an ode to the first vendors to peddle Chicago-Style Hot Tamales through the streets of Chicago:

> *Hot tamale makes you feel so jolly and gay, that's why I say*
> *But a hot tamale out of a steamin' pot,*
> *While they are nice and hot...*
> *Oh they're nice and sweet and they are good to eat.*

Undoubtedly, the Molly Man—aka the Chicago-Style Hot Tamale vendor—was a sight for sore eyes and empty bellies on cold Chicago days. Mouths watered as he reached into his steamer and unveiled a paper-wrapped tamale. Untie one end of the wrapper to reveal a yellow cornmeal cylinder. Unlike traditional tamales, which are made with masa, a white maize flour treated with lime, Chicago-style tamales are made with cornmeal.

Tom Tom has been rolling Chicago-style tamales out of its South Side factory since the 1930s. *Southern Foodways Alliance.*

The Mississippi Delta has a long-standing tamale tradition, likely the product of maize-based agriculture and a Native American culture that reaches back thousands of years. African Americans found familiarity with the dish, as it resembled cush, also known as cush-cush, a popular, savory, meat-seasoned cornmeal cake that came to the South via the African continent. The hot tamale's portability and heartiness made it the ideal meal for field workers, and African Americans carried their tamale tradition north to Chicago during the Great Migration. Indeed, most of Chicago's original Molly Men were African American. Though there is no standard Mississippi tamale recipe, with some calling for beef and others for turkey or pork, most used masa to hold the tamale together. In Chicago, the tamale adapted by taking on its yellow cornmeal and ground beef, easier ingredients to obtain in the meatpacking powerhouse that was Chicago. The Tom Tom Tamale Factory at 4750 South Washtenaw Avenue, in operation since the 1930s, offers the best Chicago-style tamales in the city, which it supplies to area restaurants and hot dog stands.

Chicago-Style Hot Tamales

3 pounds ground beef
2 tablespoons plus 1 stick butter, melted and slightly cooled
3 cups yellow cornmeal
2 tablespoons chili powder
1 tablespoon garlic powder
1 tablespoon onion powder
½ teaspoon cumin
2 tablespoons paprika
1 teaspoon cayenne pepper to taste
1 tablespoon salt
2 teaspoons sugar
Parchment paper, cut into 6- by 6-inch squares

Sauté the ground beef in 2 tablespoons of butter over medium heat until browned. Remove from heat and stir in 1 cup cornmeal and the dry spices. Set aside to cool.

In a separate bowl, combine the remaining 2 cups of cornmeal and stick of butter until thoroughly blended. Stir in just enough boiling water to make a soft dough.

Spread about 3 to 4 tablespoons of the cornmeal mixture onto each paper, making a rectangle. Place about 2 to 3 tablespoons of the seasoned meat mixture down the center of the rectangle. Fold up the bottom edge of the paper (so the cornmeal mixture wraps completely around the meat filling). Roll the tamales into the paper to produce smooth, sealed cylinders. Tie the ends of the tamales with kitchen string.

Place a colander (or metal strainer) in a large pot. Add a dash of salt and fill the pot with water up to but not touching the colander. Place the tamales into the colander, standing up, with the rolled ends at the bottom. Turn the heat to high and bring the water to a boil. As soon as the water reaches a boiling point, turn the heat down to medium-low and cover the pot with a large lid. Steam the cooking tamales for approximately 1 hour. Check the level of the water every 15 minutes, refilling with water from a pitcher as necessary. Remove the steamed tamales with kitchen tongs, one by one, and let cool for 5 minutes before serving.

ANN SATHER'S CINNAMON ROLLS WITH POWDERED SUGAR GLAZE

Warm, sweet, spiced with cinnamon and gooey with powdered sugar icing, Ann Sather's Cinnamon Rolls are the best in Chicago and more than likely the best in the world. At the eponymous Swedish American restaurant Ann Sather, which today has three city locations, you'll want to start your meal with a cinnamon bun or two or three and bring a dozen home, too, so you can indulge over the week. Though cinnamon rolls likely originated long ago in Sweden, Ann Sather perfected the recipe, making buns that are dangerously addictive.

Ann Sather's American dream came true at forty years old. When the owners of a Swedish restaurant located on Belmont Avenue in what was then a vibrant Swedish neighborhood decided to retire, Ann took a leap of faith. She quit her meatpacking plant job of twenty-two years, bought the business with her life's savings—$4,000—and opened up her dream of a diner, Ann Sather Restaurant, in 1945. Sather strived to offer wholesome comfort food that filled your belly as much as it filled your soul. She kept the former restaurant's Swedish American favorites on the menu, even though she herself was Norwegian.

Warm, sweet, spiced with cinnamon and gooey with powdered sugar icing, Ann Sather's Cinnamon Rolls are the best in Chicago and more than likely the best in the world. *Chelsea Gibson.*

Ann Sather's Cinnamon Rolls

1¼-ounce envelope active dry yeast

1 teaspoon sugar

¼ cup warm water (110° Fahrenheit)

1 cup milk, scalded, cooled

¼ cup butter, melted

⅓ cup sugar

1½ teaspoons salt

2½ to 3 cups all-purpose flour

¼ cup butter, room temperature

½ cup brown sugar

1 tablespoon cinnamon, ground

In a large bowl, stir the yeast and 1 teaspoon of sugar into the warm water and let stand for 5 minutes to soften. Stir in milk, melted butter, sugar, salt and 1 cup flour. Beat all of this with a spoon or an electric mixer until smooth. Gradually stir in 1½ cups flour, keeping the dough smooth. If the dough is still moist, stir in 1 tablespoon of flour at a time to make a soft dough. Cover with a dry cloth and let rise in a warm place until it is doubled in size, about 1 hour.

Divide the raised dough in half. On a lightly oiled board, roll out (with a lightly floured rolling pin) and stretch 1 piece of dough to make a 12- by 8-inch rectangle. Spread 2 tablespoons of the soft butter over the top of the dough. Sprinkle with brown sugar and cinnamon. Beginning on the long side, roll up tightly, jelly-roll fashion. Repeat with the remaining dough.

Cut the dough into 2-inch slices. Place on floured and greased baking sheets. Let the dough rise until doubled in bulk, about 45 minutes. Bake in a preheated 350-degree oven for 12 to 15 minutes, or until golden brown. Take the cinnamon rolls on the baking sheet out of the oven and place them to cool on a wire rack. Top the rolls with powdered sugar glaze immediately, if desired, and cool or serve warm, as you like. Makes 18 rolls.

Powdered Sugar Glaze
½ cup powdered sugar
¼ cup margarine, melted
1 teaspoon vanilla

Place all the ingredients into a small bowl and beat until creamy smooth. Glaze the cinnamon rolls immediately after taking them out of the oven. Allow the cinnamon rolls to cool on a wire rack. Serve the cinnamon rolls while still warm or cooled as you like. Makes enough to glaze 18 cinnamon rolls.

Recipe courtesy of Ann Sather

MOTHER-IN-LAWS, JUMPBALLS, JIM SHOES AND THE MAXWELL STREET POLISH

Chicago is known for its gut-busting, stick-to-your-ribs takes on classic sandwiches. Four Chicago-born sandwiches in particular—the Mother-in-Law, the Jumpball, the Jim Shoe and the Maxwell Street Polish—take the cake when it comes to overloaded, inventive sandwiches. They glorify the culinary cool that makes Chicago a place for filling your belly and lifting your spirits.

Fat Johnnie's Famous Red Hots, one of Chicago's most beloved hot dog institutions located at 7242 South Western Avenue, claims on its charming retro sign that its foodstuffs are "Fit for a King." It also lays claim to inventing the Mother-in-Law, an overloaded sandwich that can wipe out hangovers and rev you up for either a long afternoon on the job or a long afternoon nap. Fat Johnnie's owner, John Pawlikowski, remembered buying a tamale stuffed in a hot dog bun for a nickel from a pushcart vendor when he was a child. The vendor referred to the mouthwatering sandwich as a Mother-in-Law. The savory sandwich made such an impression on Pawikowski that he added it to the menu of Fat Johnnie's when he opened it in 1972. Indeed, Fat Johnnie's Mother-in-Law sandwich is certainly the stuff of royalty: a Chicago-style hot tamale topped with chili rests comfortably in a steamed hot dog bun. While most places leave the Mother-in-Law alone, Fat Johnnie's loads her up with the usual Chicago-Style Hot Dog condiments. Some say she was inspired by the torta de tamal, a bolillo—Mexico's baguette—filled with a Mexican-style tamale.

Fat Johnnie's Mother-in-Law sandwich is certainly the stuff of royalty: a Chicago-style hot tamale topped with chili rests comfortably in a steamed hot dog bun and arrives loaded with the usual Chicago-Style Hot Dog condiments. *Southern Foodways Alliance.*

Also on Western Avenue, at 16 South, Moon's Sandwich is the home of yet another over-the-top Chicago sandwich: the Jumpball. Step up to the old-school diner countertop and watch as three eggs are scrambled before your eyes on the griddle, with onions, potatoes and savory Italian sausage. American cheese is added to fuse the ingredients together before they're cradled between two slices of toast. It's the quintessential breakfast sandwich, though it's perfect for any time of day. Moon's has been serving its Jumpball since it opened in 1933. Word has it that Moon's also served a side of moonshine during Prohibition, hence its name.

A Jim Shoe is a stacked sandwich layered with gyros, corned and roast beef, lettuce and tomato, then topped with tzatziki and nestled in a toasted Italian baguette. No one knows exactly who invented it, but it pops up on menus and plates across the city. And you'll find this particular Jim Shoe only in Chicago.

A Maxwell Street Polish calls for Polish sausage. Made with both pork and beef, nestled in a bun and topped with grilled onions and a stripe of yellow mustard, it is a Chicago-specific variation of kielbasa distinguished by it being typically more seasoned and made from a combination of both beef and pork. Though you can find Maxwell Street Polish citywide today, the best

Above: Moon's Sandwich Shop has been serving its Jumpball since it opened in 1933. Word has it that it also served a side of moonshine during Prohibition, hence the name Moon's. *Chelsea Gibson.*

Left: The Jumpball, Chicago's quintessential breakfast sandwich.

place to find the sandwich is at Jim's Original (1250 South Union Avenue), an iconic hot dog stand that opened in 1939, when Jimmy Stefanovic, an emigrant from Macedonia, took over his aunt and uncle's hot dog stand and

Jim Shoe sandwich: layered with gyros, corned and roast beef, lettuce and tomato, then topped with tzatziki and nestled in a toasted Italian baguette. *Chelsea Gibson.*

Though you can find Maxwell Street Polish citywide today, the best place to find the sandwich is at Jim's Original (1250 South Union Avenue), an iconic hot dog stand that opened in 1939, when Jimmy Stefanovic, an emigrant from Macedonia, took over his aunt and uncle's hot dog stand and named it after none other than himself. *Chelsea Gibson.*

named it after none other than himself. Though Jim's Original lays claim to having created the sandwich, it was likely the first brick-and-mortar stand to sell the sandwich, which was likely pushcart peddled years before on the streets of Chicago's Maxwell Street Market.

Though you can easily assemble your Mother-in-Law, Jumpball or Maxwell Street Polish at home, your best bet is to head to one of these three beloved Chicago institutions. After a hard day's work or a long night of partying, there is nothing quite like the smells and flavors of the classic Chicago greasy spoon diner or stand cooking up a sandwich that you know will fill your tummy, heart and soul.

SUBGUM

Subgum is a Cantonese American dish that first appeared in Chicago around the turn of the century, a time when Chicago already boasted several Chinese restaurants. The *Chicago Daily Tribune* included subgum in a list of popular Chinese American dishes in 1902, while John Drury's 1931 *Dining in Chicago* guide shows that it was a popular main course at many established Chinese restaurants. Subgum, which translates to "numerous and varied" in Cantonese, is a simple dish that appealed to the budding American love affair with Chinese food. Stir-fried chicken and vegetables—carrots, celery and water chestnuts—are nestled atop crunchy, deep-fried noodles. You won't find it on a menu in China, and it's uncommon to find it on menus in Chinese restaurants in other parts of the United States, but subgum remains a popular dish in many Chinese American restaurants in Chicago.

One of the best spots to enjoy subgum is at Chicago's very own Orange Garden, the second-oldest Chinese restaurant in the city. Located at 1942 West Irving Park Road in the North Center neighborhood, this classic Chinese American eatery was opened in 1926 by a certain W. Chan. Chan successfully melded classic American Art Deco diner décor with Chinese accents. Likewise, the dishes on the menu here—egg foo young, sweet and sour pork, kung pao chicken and, of course, subgum—are all Americanized takes on traditional Cantonese cuisine. Orange Garden's neon sign, said to be the oldest in the city, advertises chop suey in glowing emerald green.

Above: Subgum, which translates to "numerous and varied" in Cantonese, is a simple dish that appealed to the budding American love affair with Chinese food.

Left: One of the best spots to enjoy subgum is at Chicago's very own Orange Garden, the second-oldest Chinese restaurant in the city. Located at 1942 West Irving Park Road in the North Center neighborhood, this classic Chinese American eatery has been serving Chicagoans since 1926.

Subgum sets itself apart from chop suey thanks to one missing ingredient: there are no bean sprouts in subgum. Play around with the veggies—this recipe is a good excuse to clear out the fridge at the end of the week.

Subgum

½ cup vegetable oil
3 cloves of garlic, peeled and chopped
1 onion, peeled and diced
4 chicken breasts, cut into small, stir-fry-sized pieces
1 cup broccoli
1 cup pea pods
1 cup mushrooms
1 cup chopped celery
1 can water chestnuts
2 cups chicken broth
2 tablespoons cornstarch
Crispy chow mein noodles

Heat oil in wok. Add garlic and onion and stir fry until onion is soft. Add chicken and stir fry until cooked. Add vegetables and stir fry until cooked. Mix together chicken broth and cornstarch in a separate bowl, add to the wok and stir fry until mixture thickens. Serve over crispy chow mein noodles.

THE RAINBOW CONE AND PALMER HOUSE ICE CREAM

Joseph Sapp grew up in Ohio as an orphan on a work farm. Whenever he managed to save up a few pennies, he would treat himself to a simple ice cream cone, dreaming of the day when he could afford a giant cone piled with scoops of every flavor under the rainbow. As an adult, he worked as a Buick mechanic by day and aspiring ice cream maker by night. In 1926, he opened Original Rainbow Cone, together with his wife, Katherine. Always

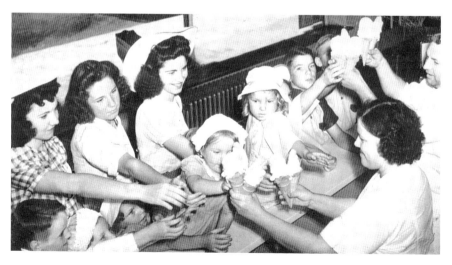

Cheers to Original Rainbow Cone, a Chicago summertime classic since 1926. *Original Rainbow Cone.*

Stacked with horizontal layers of chocolate, strawberry, Palmer House, pistachio and orange sherbet atop a wafer cone, the Original Rainbow Cone is an iconic Chicago treat. *Original Rainbow Cone.*

forward thinking, Sapp chose to build his shop at the corner of Ninety-Second Street and Western Avenue, correctly predicting that Western Avenue would soon become a major roadway as Chicago extended farther south. Today, Original Rainbow Cone stands as one of Chicago's oldest ice cream shops.

Stacked with horizontal layers of chocolate, strawberry, Palmer House, pistachio and orange sherbet atop a wafer cone, the Original Rainbow Cone is an iconic Chicago treat. Driving down Western Avenue on Chicago's far South Side neighborhood of Beverly, you'll know you've arrived when you spot the giant ice cream cone that stands as a beacon on the rooftop of this candy floss pink ice cream palace. On summer nights, there will likely be a line out the door as customers wait for a Rainbow Cone, which always comes complete with a few spoonfuls of nostalgia, too.

When Sapp developed his original rainbow of flavors, he invented Palmer House ice cream, a creamy vanilla dotted with toasted walnuts and sweet cherries. He named his fancy new flavor after the chicest hotel in 1920s Chicago: the Palmer House. If you want to make your very own Rainbow Cone at home, you'll have to make your own Palmer House ice cream, which is best served sandwiched between strawberry and pistachio.

Palmer House Ice Cream

2 cups heavy cream
1 cup whole milk
¾ cup sugar
1 tablespoon pure vanilla extract
Pinch kosher salt
1 cup of frozen cherries
⅔ cup toasted chopped walnuts.

Whisk the cream, milk and sugar in a bowl until sugar is completely dissolved. Stir in the vanilla extract and salt. Add the cherries and walnuts. Pour the mixture into an ice cream maker and churn according to the manufacturer's instructions. Transfer to a freezer-safe container and freeze for at least 2 hours before serving.

CHICAGO-STYLE DEEP DISH PIZZA

Chicago-Style Deep Dish Pizza is more a decadent pie than a plain old pizza. It's the grand poohbah of pizza, a beloved, decadent Chicago icon. Whether it's served in a pan, stuffed or simply stacked with mozzarella cheese, then topped with a chunky tomato sauce, it's the thick, tall, golden crust that makes it one of the best pizza pies in the world.

Though its exact origins are murky, Pizzeria Uno claims to be the birthplace of Chicago-Style Deep Dish Pizza. In 1943, former University of Texas football star Ike Sewell and World War II vet Ric Riccardo opened up Pizzeria Uno in an elegant Victorian mansion that once belonged to lumber magnate Nathan Mears at the corner of Wabash and Ohio. The duo dreamed up a thicker, buttery-crustier, cheesier version of the classic pizza recipe that would set their pizzas apart from the rest. Their deep-dish pizzas were such a hit that by 1955, they had opened a second location one block north: the aptly named Pizzeria Due.

Pizzeria Uno set the standard for Chicago-style pizza, which must meet two criteria to be classified so. The crust must be sweeter and more pastry-like than a standard pizza crust and the cheese abundant. It takes longer to bake a deep dish pizza—about an hour—so cornmeal is sprinkled in the large pan to insulate the crust, and a thicker layer of toppings protects the cheese as it slowly melts. Because of this, wait times are longer, though you can always count on an unforgettably delicious pizza, piping hot and oozing with cheese, arriving at your table in a few minutes under an hour. Plan on eating this hearty pie with a knife and a fork.

Luciano "Lou" Malnati started out as a young bartender at Pizzeria Uno and then moved up and onward to manage Pizzeria Due. Later, in 1971, he opened a pizzeria of his very own, now a chain managed by his sons, Marc and Rick. "Chicago-Style Deep Dish Pizza is the heartiest of the pizza varieties and typically eaten with a knife and fork," explains Marc Malnati. "The dough is patted out by hand and raised up high on the sides of a seasoned deep dish pizza pan. The crust complements the toppings, not allowing any ingredients to dominate another."

There are two other variations to the classic Chicago-Style Deep Dish Pizza: stuffed and pan. Giordano's perfected the stuffed pizza, which truly is a pie. A second layer of dough is

Top: In 1943, former University of Texas football star Ike Sewell and his pal World War II vet Ric Riccardo opened their Pizzeria Uno in an elegant Victorian mansion that once belonged to lumber magnate Nathan Mears at the corner of Wabash and Ohio. *Pizzeria Uno.*

Left: Pizzeria Uno set the standard for Chicago-style pizza, which must meet two criteria to be classified so. The crust must be sweeter and more pastry-like than a standard pizza crust and the cheese abundant. *Pizzeria Uno.*

placed above the standard deep dish pizza, which is then topped with more sauce and parmesan cheese. The two buttery crusts hold cheese or additional toppings in the center. Efren and Joseph Boglio opened the first Giordano's in 1973, and their stuffed deep dish pizza was inspired by Northern Italian–style pizza rustica, traditionally served at Easter time and baked by Mama Giordano in their family's native Torino.

Attributed to Connie's Pizza, a chain that started on the South Side when Jim Stolfe traded in his prized 1962 Oldsmobile Starfire to open his first restaurant in Bridgeport in 1963, pan pizza is all about the dough. "While most deep dish pizzas feature dense, buttery crust similar to pie crust, Connie's uses a tender bread dough, similar to focaccia bread, with a good amount of oil and high hydration levels," explains Connie's owner Mike Stolfe. "We believe in using a little less dough and a little more love. The dough goes through a thirty-hour fermentation process that makes it [more tender] and allows the flavor to develop more. It's made fresh nightly so it can go through the fermentation process and be ready for the next day. In addition to using premium dough, the toppings are added after the sauce rather than before like other deep dish pizzas."

Pan pizza sets itself apart by using a special method to prep and bake the deep dish pizza's dough and is attributed to Connie's Pizza, a chain that started on the South Side when Jim Stolfe traded in his prized 1962 Oldsmobile Starfire to open his first restaurant in Bridgeport in 1963. *Connie's Pizza.*

"While most deep dish pizzas feature dense, buttery crust similar to pie crust, Connie's uses a tender bread dough, similar to focaccia bread, with a good amount of oil and high hydration levels," explains Connie's owner Mike Stolfe. "We believe in using a little less dough and a little more love." *Connie's Pizza.*

"Chicago deep dish pizza is a style that few people outside of [Chicago] truly understand," shares Jonathan Porter of Chicago Pizza Tours. "It's a style that has remained unique to Chicago and is enjoyed by locals and visitors alike. There's nothing quite like digging into a delectable deep dish Chicago-style pizza."

Chicago-Style Deep Dish Pizza

Crust

1 cup warm water

3 teaspoons instant yeast

4 cups flour

½ cup ground yellow cornmeal

1 teaspoon salt

¼ cup olive oil

¼ cup butter, melted

Filling

14-ounce can diced plum tomatoes, drained
2 teaspoons mixed dried Italian herbs
4 garlic cloves, peeled and minced
Salt to taste
1 pound mozzarella cheese, sliced
1 pound Italian sausage, cooked and sliced
1 cup freshly grated parmesan

Preheat the oven to 425° Fahrenheit. Pour the warm water into a large mixing bowl and stir in yeast until it is dissolved. Add the other dough ingredients and knead by hand until you have a smooth ball of dough. Place the dough in a buttered bowl, cover and let rise until it has doubled in size (about 1 hour). Knead the dough again for about 5 minutes, then press it into a deep dish pizza pan that has been greased with butter and 2 tablespoons of olive oil. Set the crust by baking for 10 minutes.

Prepare the sauce by seasoning the tomatoes with the dried Italian herbs, garlic and salt to taste. Cover the bottom of the crust with the sliced mozzarella. Add the sausage and, finally, the sauce. Sprinkle with parmesan and drizzle with the remaining olive oil. Bake the pizza for 25 minutes, then lower the temperature to 400° and bake for about 10 more minutes, or until golden brown. Allow the pizza to cool for about 15 minutes before cutting and serving with a large spatula.

SHRIMP DE JONGHE

The De Jonghe Hotel was the place to be during Chicago's Roaring Twenties. Socialites—Mrs. Edith Rockefeller McCormick and Mrs. Potter Palmer were frequent diners—stars and politicians mingled at the in-house restaurant at 12 East Monroe Street.

The De Jonghe brothers, immigrants to Chicago from Belgium, found success with their very first restaurant, which they opened at the 1892 World's Columbian Exposition. By 1899, they had opened their eponymous hotel and restaurant. Their signature dish, Shrimp De Jonghe, a garlicky, herbed shrimp casserole with a dash of nutmeg, was a sensation in the city and beyond.

Shrimp De Jonghe is a product of its time. Garlic was considered almost exotic—or at least American tastes, accustomed to largely bland food, were just beginning to turn to the odiferous onion variety. Shrimp was another exotic ingredient. By the time it arrived in restaurant kitchens, it may not have always been as fresh as it is today, hence the dish is herbed to the max.

Though the famed restaurant didn't survive Prohibition—a headwaiter offered to serve a Prohibition agent three bottles of whiskey and a raid ensued—its acclaimed, sherry-spiked Shrimp De Jonghe survived and remains a beloved dish featured in Chicago.

While the recipe for Shrimp De Jonghe is usually credited to Henri De Jonghe, affectionately referred to by many as PaPa De Jonghe, some clues point to the restaurant's chef, Emil Zehr, as the actual inventor. When the *Chicago Tribune* printed a recipe for the "original" Shrimp De Jonghe in the mid-1980s, Emil Zehr Jr. wrote in, protesting that his father had invented the dish and noting that

"Dad would never have used liquor in his recipe." He added, "There have been a lot of recipes published, but only this is the original." The recipe below is an adaption of Zehr's original recipe, which his son shared with the *Tribune*.

Shrimp De Jongue

4 cups homemade white bread crumbs

3 pounds butter, softened

⅓ cup chopped shallots

1 tablespoon Worcestershire sauce

1 ounce good dry sherry (fino, manzanilla or amontillado)

3 drops liquid hot pepper sauce

1 cup chopped fresh garlic

1 cup chopped parsley

12 large shrimp, peeled and cleaned

1 lemon

1 bay leaf

1 teaspoon sea salt

Preheat oven to 375° Fahrenheit. In a food processor, make your bread crumbs from French or Italian bread that is 3 days old. This has a great deal to do with its fine texture when finished.

Mix the butter and all other ingredients (except shrimp, lemon, bay leaf and sea salt) in a wooden bowl. Form into a sausage and place in refrigerator to set, about a half hour.

Cook the shrimp by filling a large-sized saucepan with water, the juice of 1 lemon, the bay leaf and the sea salt. Bring to a boil. Add the shrimp; cover and simmer for 2 minutes, until the shrimp are barely pink. Do not overcook (the shrimp will not be completely cooked). Drain shrimp immediately, running them under cool tap water for 30 seconds.

Cover bottom of casserole with ⅛-inch slices of the butter mixture. Place the shrimp on top of the butter mixture slices. Cover shrimp with ¼-inch slices of butter mixture. Bake until the bread crumbs are golden brown, about 10 minutes.

CHICAGO-BORN COCKTAILS
Chicago Fizz, Chicago Cocktail, Cohasset Punch

In the short foreword to his classic 1917 tome *The Ideal Bartender*, Tom Bullock, a St. Louis bartender and the first African American to publish a cocktail recipe book, mused, "Is it any wonder that mankind stands

Widely considered an American invention, it wasn't until Prohibition ended in 1933 that cocktail lounges began to sprout up across Chicago, replacing the traditional, beer- and straight hard liquor–focused saloons. *Chelsea Gibson.*

Chicago-born cocktails reimagined by mixologist Doug Phillips at the Heavy Feather (Second Floor, 2357 North Milwaukee Avenue): Chicago Cocktail, Chicago Fizz, Cohasset Punch and Mickey Finn. *Chelsea Gibson.*

open-mouthed before the bartender, considering the mysteries and marvels of an art that borders on magic?" Widely considered an American invention, it wasn't until Prohibition ended in 1933 that cocktail lounges began to sprout up across Chicago, replacing the traditional, beer- and straight hard liquor–focused saloons, elevating the bartender to cocktail craftsman/magician.

Though their origins are as a foggy as one feels after a couple strong cocktails, the Chicago Fizz, Chicago Cocktail and Cohasset Punch all have ties to the Windy City. The Mickey Finn, now slang for any doctored, potent cocktail, was mixed into life in a pre–cocktail era Chicago saloon.

The original recipes, featured here, have been reimagined for the twenty-first century by Doug Phillips, mixologist and beverage director for the classic Logan Square '70s fern bar, the Heavy Feather (Second Floor, 2357 North Milwaukee Avenue).

CHICAGO FIZZ

The origins of the Chicago Fizz are murky. What we do know is that this effervescent cocktail traveled from Chicago to New York City's Waldorf-Astoria bar. In barman Albert S. Crockett's *The Old Waldorf Astoria Bar Book* (1935), he notes that the cocktail is "an importation from the Windy City long before bombs, machine guns and sawed-off shotguns had come to disturb its peaceful life."

Chicago Fizz

The Old Waldorf Astoria Bar Book, *Albert S. Crockett (1935)*

Juice from ¼ lemon
½ spoon sugar
1 egg white
½ jigger Jamaican rum
½ jigger port wine

Ice. Shake. Strain. Fill from siphon.

Chicago Fizz Revisited

1½ ounces El Dorado 5-year rum
¾ ounce ruby port
½ ounce lemon juice
½ ounce clove syrup*
Egg whites
Soda water

Combine all ingredients and shake vigorously. Serve in a Collins glass with no ice and top with soda water. Garnish with a strip of angostura bitters.

*Clove Syrup

Put ¼ cup of cloves in a sauce pan and heat up until toasted. Combine 1 quart of fine sugar, 1 quart of water and the toasted clove and bring to a boil. Once boiling, let the syrup reduce for 5 minutes and remove from heat. Strain away the cloves.

CHICAGO COCKTAIL

C*hicago Daily News* reporter John Drury included the recipe for this fine dessert cocktail in his 1931 guide, *Dining in Chicago*, noting that it had been served at the American Bar in Nice and the Embassy Club in London. It also appeared in the 1930 *Savoy Cocktail Book*.

Chicago Cocktail
Dining in Chicago, *John Drury (1931)*

Fill the mixing glass half full of broken ice. Add 1 or 2 dashes of angostura bitters, 3 dashes of curacao and ½ a gill (1 ounce) of brandy. Stir well and strain into a cocktail glass. Add an olive or cherry, squeeze a lemon peel and drop it into the glass and pour a little champagne on top. Before straining the mixture in the cocktail glass, moisten the outside borders of the glass with lemon juice and dip into pulverized sugar.

Chicago Cocktail Revisited

¾ ounce Rhine Hall Mango Brandy (locally produced at
  Rhine Hall Distillery, 2010 West Fulton Street)
¾ ounce Blanco tequila
¼ ounce orange curacao
¼ ounce lime juice
1 bar spoon simple syrup
2 dashes Peychaud's bitters
Sparkling wine

Before building the cocktail, rim a champagne flute with salt
by taking a lime wedge and rubbing it along the outer rim
and then dunking the rim in a plate of salt. Lightly shake all
ingredients other than sparkling wine and pour into the salt-
rimmed champagne flute. Top with sparkling wine.

COHASSET PUNCH

Though it is considered a Chicago-born cocktail, Cohasset Punch was actually first concocted in the eponymous Massachusetts bayside town. Gus Williams, a Chicago bartender-for-hire, created the drink for his employer, popular actor William H. Crane (1845–1928), a celebrity in his time. The cocktail made its debut at a Gatsby-esque Cohasset party hosted by Crane. Sweet with a hidden, packed punch that hits you after one or two, Williams's cocktail was such a hit that by 1916, he was able to sell his one-of-a-kind recipe to Ladner Bros., a saloon at 207 West Madison Avenue. After Prohibition, Ladner Bros. built its business on the popular punch. Its once iconic sign even featured an East Coast lighthouse, while "Home of Cohasset Punch" flashed in pink neon.

The first recipe for Cohasset Punch appears in *The Ideal Bartender* (1917), a collection of cocktail recipes compiled by St. Louis bartender Tom Bullock.

Cohasset Punch

The Ideal Bartender, *Tom Bullock (1917)*

1 jigger New England rum
1 jigger vermouth
3 dashes gum syrup
1 dash orange bitters
Juice of ½ lemon

Fill one large bar glass ½ full of shaved ice. Add ingredients, stir and serve with a preserved peach and its liquor.

Cohasset Punch Revisted

1 ounce Cruzan Blackstrap Rum
1 ounce Bank Note Blended Scotch
½ ounce Brovo Lucky Falernum
½ ounce Bonal Quinquina
½ ounce lemon juice
¼ ounce passion fruit syrup (modern substitute for peach)

Combine all ingredients and shake. Serve the cocktail in a double old fashioned glass over ice.

MICKEY FINN

Mickey Finn was the manager of the Lone Star Saloon and Palm Garden, which stood on Whiskey Row, the saloon-stacked west side of State Street that ran from Van Buren to Harrison, in the late 1800s. Some say Mickey Finn was from Ireland and others Peoria. It appears that he made his dastardly debut in Chicago at the 1893 World's Fair, where he earned his living as a lush worker, robbing drunken fairgoers. Later, he worked as a pickpocket. With his earnings, he was able to open his saloon, which also operated as a pickpocket training academy. His "Mickey Finn Special" was such a notorious cocktail that the slang term "Mickey Finn" still refers to any drug-laced drink today.

The best account of Finn's life comes from Herbert Asbury's *Gem of the Prairie* (1940). According to Asbury, in 1898, Finn met a voodoo doctor named Hall who sold quack potions and cocaine, among other wares, to the bawdy houses around town. From Hall, Finn procured a large brown bottle filled with a concoction that contained chloral hydrate. "Gold Tooth" Mary, one of Finn's house girls (ladies employed to encourage the men to drink up and more), would later testify that Finn presented the bottle to her and exclaimed, "We'll get the money with this! I give the doc an extra dollar to make it strong!" Indeed, Finn put a sign up at the bar advertising the "Mickey Finn Special," a cocktail containing grain alcohol, snuff-infused water and Hall's potion.

"When the victims drank this dopey stuff," testified Gold Tooth Mary, "they get talkative, walk around in a restless manner and then fall into a deep sleep, and you can't arouse them until the effect of the drug wears off."

A trip to Maurice Lenell's former cookie factory on Harlem Avenue in Norridge was once a childhood rite of passage. To see the cookies tumble down the conveyor belt, fresh from the oven, was delightful; to be able to eat as many broken cookies as you wanted was nothing short of heavenly. While the company was known for its many cookie types— chocolate chip, English toffee, jelly stars—Maurice Lenell's pinwheels, with their chocolate and vanilla swirls and pink sugared edges, were the stars. *Molly Smith.*

Ann Sather's American dream came true at forty years old. When the owners of a Swedish restaurant located in what was then a vibrant Swedish neighborhood on Belmont Avenue decided to retire, Ann took a leap of faith. She quit her meatpacking plant job of twenty-two years, bought the business with her life's savings ($4,000) and opened up her dream of a diner, Ann Sather Restaurant, in 1945. *Ann Sather.*

Connie's Pizza, a chain that started on the South Side when Jim Stolfe traded in his prized 1962 Oldsmobile Starfire to open his first restaurant in Bridgeport in 1963, now delivers its beloved pan pizzas across the city. *Connie's Pizza.*

During the World's Columbian Exposition of 1893, Bertha Palmer worked with the Palmer House pastry chef to create a delicious dessert that would be compact enough to fit into a boxed lunch for attending ladies. The result was the rich, chocolaty, yet small and less crumbly brownie, a small square that was big on taste yet offered a more elegant eating experience for ladies on the move. *Palmer House.*

The original recipe for Bookbinder Soup, created in 1893 by Samuel Bookbinder of the eponymous Old Original Bookbinder's restaurant in Philadelphia, was gifted to the Drake to celebrate its inauguration. Over the years, the recipe for this savory, tomato-based vegetable soup was adapted by the Cape Cod Room. The biggest change occurred when snapping turtle was replaced with red snapper. *Chelsea Gibson.*

Fannie May Pixies—fresh, crunchy pecans smothered in a buttery caramel and drenched in silky-smooth chocolate—were first created just after World War II. *Fannie May.*

The four-inch, think-skinned Melrose peppers grown with love by the Italian American community in Chicagoland are rich and flavorful and best served stuffed with Italian spices, sausages and cheeses that complement their sweetness. *Marie Renello from ProudItalianCook.com.*

The Liakouras brothers, founders of Greektown's Parthenon Restaurant, offered a free saganaki to every diner, drawing in their first customers with their dazzling new dish. The restaurant, which today is run by Chris Liakouras's daughter, claims, "Before saganaki was flambéed here, it was merely fried cheese." *Parthenon*.

Hidden in the shadow of the El's Brown line, in a classic 1870s wood-frame house, Gene & Georgetti was the realization of the American dream for partners Gene Michelotti and Alfredo "Georgetti" Federighi. While working as a bartender, Michelotti encountered his future business partner, Federighi, who was working as a chef. In 1941, Gene & Georgetti opened its doors, with Alfredo manning the kitchen and Gene working the front and holding down the bar. *Chelsea Gibson.*

As John Drury said, "Whatever its origin, cocktail drinking is an old American custom. It has been truly said that what wine is to a Frenchman, whiskey to an Englishman, beer to a German, the cocktail is to the American." *Chelsea Gibson.*

Chicago Daily News reporter John Drury included the recipe for the Chicago Cocktail, a fine dessert cocktail, in his 1931 guide, *Dining in Chicago*, noting that it had been served at the American Bar in Nice and the Embassy Club in London. It also appeared in the 1930 *Savoy Cocktail Book*. *Chelsea Gibson.*

Right: In 1864, Phillip Henrici, the son of Viennese restaurateurs, immigrated to New York, where he began his career working as a baker's apprentice. He moved to Chicago in 1868, opening a small diner at 71 North State Street, where he served coffee, sandwiches and pastries. He advertised, "All you can eat for a quarter." Three fried eggs cost fifteen cents and apple pie, five cents. *New York Public Library Digital Archives.*

Below: From carts scattered throughout the city, both newly arrived and established Chicagoans realized their small piece of the American dream by starting fledgling businesses via their hot dog carts. *Chelsea Gibson.*

"How to Make a Chicago Hot Dog." *Graphic Courtesy of Vienna Beef.*

In 1955, Luciano "Lou" Malnati started out as a young bartender at Pizzeria Uno and then moved up and onward to manage Pizzeria Due. Later, he opened a pizzeria of his very own, now a chain managed by his sons, Marc and Rick. "Chicago-Style Deep Dish Pizza is the heartiest of the pizza varieties and typically eaten with a knife and fork," explains Marc Malnati.

Lou Margie's Candies has been placing cherries atop sundaes and life since 1921, when Peter George Poulos opened an ice cream parlor on the corner of Milwaukee and Armitage. It wasn't officially called Margie's Candies until 1933, when George married his sweetheart, Margie Michaels. *Chelsea Gibson.*

When little Mario DiPaolo was in kindergarten in the late 1940s, he was so rambunctious that his parents decided to put his energy to work. Mario's dad parked a shaved ice maker in front of their little storefront on Taylor Street, and Mario happily hand-cranked his way to fame. *Chelsea Gibson.*

Orange Sherbet

Pistachio

Palmer House (New York Vanilla with cherries and walnuts)

Strawberry

Chocolate

THE ORIGINAL
RAINBOW CONE
EST. 1926

Left: Anatomy of an Original Rainbow Cone. *Original Rainbow Cone.*

Below: Though they were born in Poland in the Middle Ages, pączki (pronounced "poonch-key"), traditional Polish filled donuts symbolizing the start of Lent, are a beloved Fat Tuesday tradition in Chicago. Chicago-style pączki take the fillings to another level altogether, piping in everything from passion fruit jelly to whiskey chocolate to PB&J. The more creative, the better. *Delightful Pastries.*

Above: A Maxwell Street Polish calls for a Polish sausage. Made with both pork and beef, nestled in a bun and topped with grilled onions and a stripe of yellow mustard, it's a Chicago-specific variation of kielbasa distinguished by it being typically more seasoned and made from a combination of both beef and pork. *Chelsea Gibson.*

Right: Pullman's dining cars were known for their exceptional cuisine. Raw oysters, roast spring lamb with mint sauce, fricandeu of veal à la macedoine, venison steaks and lobster salad were among the menu choices, all served with the finest wines, champagnes, whiskeys, brandies, beers and ales from around the world. Sublime service was provided by the Pullman porters, African American men who fought hard for respect, formed the first black labor union and were an integral part of the passenger railroad industry. *New York Public Library Digital Archives.*

Efren and Joseph Boglio opened the first Giordano's in 1973, and their stuffed deep dish pizza was inspired by the pizza rustica, traditionally served at Easter time and baked by Mama Giordano in their family's native Torino. *Giordano's.*

Subgum is a Cantonese American dish that first appeared in Chicago around the turn of the century, a time when Chicago boasted roughly 167 Chinese restaurants. In 1902, the *Chicago Daily Tribune* included subgum in a list of popular Chinese American dishes in 1902, while John Drury's 1931 *Dining in Chicago* guide showed that it was a popular main course at many established Chinese restaurants. *Chelsea Gibson.*

Right: Since it opened in the late 1920s, Chicago's Swedish Bakery has been baking up delectable pastries made with cardamom, saffron, anise, fennel, orange peel and almond paste—the spices of Sweden. The store's most popular item is its Andersonville Coffee Cake, a wreath-shaped coffee cake with a black cardamom–spiked dough and a sweet almond and cinnamon filling. *Chelsea Gibson.*

Below: Ann Sather strived to offer wholesome comfort food that filled your belly as much as it filled her soul. Though cinnamon rolls likely originated long ago in Sweden, Ann Sather perfected the recipe, making buns that are dangerously addictive. *Ann Sather.*

The Italian beef sandwich is not just a Chicago-born and bred favorite; it's also an icon. Born out of the Great Depression, the Italian beef sandwich calls for lean and tougher cuts of meat. Cooked for several hours, then sliced super thin and served on a big roll drenched in the beef's spiced cooking juices, this is a sandwich that stretches the meaty flavor while also filling up your belly. *Wikimedia.*

Anyone who's anyone in the city of Chicago has sneaked in for Margie's sundaes. Al Capone enjoyed the Black Walnut Sundae, while the Beatles dug into an Atomic Sundae.

Right: When a kindly Marshall Field's clerk, Mrs. Herring, shared her lunch with a tired shopper, a light bulb went off. Marshall Field, whose famous slogan was "Give the lady what she wants," recognized the need to better accommodate his female customers and, in turn, increase sales. Perennial favorite Mrs. Herring's Chicken Pot Pie remains a Walnut Room favorite. *Courtesy of Macy's.*

Below: Retro Green River ad. *John Wondrasek.*

"Here in Chicago, we up the ante, adding more chiles and skipping a few of the ingredients found in a traditional Italian sottoaceto," shares Chicago-based foodie John Amici. "The result is more condiment than antipasto, and it's a staple of most 'reputable' sandwich shops. In fact, in some circles, it's almost sacrilege to order an Italian beef sandwich without a healthy scoop of giardiniera to top it off—but that's not all. Good giardiniera makes a great topping for any sandwich, as well as for burgers, hot dogs and brats, while a healthy sprinkling of it can elevate even the most lackluster of pizzas." *John Amici.*

Roeser's is best known for its German chocolate cake, a moist, delicious dessert composed of devil's food chocolate sponge cake layered with a decadent pecan and coconut flake filling. Contrary to popular belief, German chocolate cake doesn't originate from Germany; rather, it originated in Dorchester, Massachusetts, where American chocolate maker Samuel German formulated the baking chocolate used in his namesake recipe. Roeser's perfected the recipe here in Chicago, making the cake even more decadent. *Chelsea Gibson.*

Finn called the rear of his saloon his "operating room"; it was there that the victims were dragged and pockets emptied. Sometimes, Finn even went so far as to strip them of their clothes if they were of good enough quality. The victims awoke, usually in an alley, unable to remember the course of events that had gotten them into such a terrible predicament. Mary also testified that Finn boasted he'd never be arrested because he paid the police for protection and had a tight pact with his aldermen, "Hinky Dink" Mike Kenna and "Bath House" John Coughlin. The police raided the saloon only after Gold Tooth Mary, who came to regret her role in the scheme and feared Finn would murder her for the money she'd managed to save up, testified before an aldermanic graft commission, but by the time they conducted the raid, they found only a few bottles of body lotion and cough syrup. Still, Finn lost his saloon license, and the Lone Star closed in 1903. He left Chicago for a few months but returned to sell his alleged poisonous potion recipe to a few off-the-radar criminal barkeepers.

Doug Phillips's take on the Mickey Finn packs a powerfully pleasant punch but won't knock you out like the original.

Mickey Finn Revisited

2 ounces Old Grand Dad, 114-proof navy strength
¾ ounce Cocchi di Torino
¼ ounce Green Chartreuse, 109 proof
Spray of tobacco tincture* to replace snuff

Add all ingredients in a mixing glass and stir. Serve the cocktail in a double old fashioned glass.

*Tobacco Tincture
Take 3 grams of whole leaf tobacco and add it to a bottle of high-proof neutral grain spirit (e.g., Everclear). Store at room temperature for at least 24 hours; the longer you wait, the more tobacco flavor you have.

ELI'S CHEESECAKE

Made in Chicago with premium ingredients, Eli's cheesecakes are the best in the city and beyond. They've been the sweet, celebratory dessert for many a Chicago birthday and anniversary, but they also make for a sweet single-spoon indulgence on a rainy Monday afternoon or a late Friday night fridge raid. Known as "Chicago's most famous dessert," Eli's cheesecakes have been served at everything from the city's 150th birthday party to four American presidential inaugurations.

The story of Eli's Cheesecake began with Eli Schulman, who opened his first restaurant in 1940: Eli's Ogden Huddle on Chicago's West Side. During World War II, Eli hung a sign in the window: "If you are hungry and have no money, we will feed you free." Perhaps his giving spirit toward the citizens of Chicago was what drew outstanding success his way. He later opened Eli's, The Place for Steak in Chicago's Streeterville neighborhood, and it soon became the stomping grounds for celebrities, sports stars and politicians, including Frank Sinatra, football legend Gale Sayers and President Bill Clinton. Eli's Cheesecake was born at Eli's, The Place for Steak but made its second grand debut at the first Taste of Chicago, the city's famous foodie festival, on July 4, 1980.

Eli's Cheesecake became so famous that it has its very own world. Eli's Cheesecake World in Chicago's Dunning neighborhood is a corporate office, bakery, retail store and dessert café all wrapped up into one sweet destination. Top-notch ingredients like pure Madagascar vanilla and Ida red apples from Michigan set Eli's cheesecakes—which come in dozens of flavors—apart from

Known as "Chicago's most famous dessert," Eli's cheesecakes have been served at everything from the city's 150th birthday party to four American presidential inaugurations. *Image courtesy of Eli's Cheesecake.*

the rest. Each cake is slow baked in small batches, hand decorated and certified kosher. Hundreds of cakes roll out of the ovens here daily, after which they're delivered throughout Chicago, across the United States and around the world.

"Almost Eli's" Cheesecake

4 packages (8 ounces each) cream cheese, softened
1 cup sugar
2 tablespoons all-purpose flour
2 large eggs
1 egg yolk
6 tablespoons sour cream
½ teaspoon vanilla
Graham crust (see page 100)

Heat oven to 350° Fahrenheit. Beat cream cheese, sugar and flour in mixing bowl of an electric mixer until light and creamy. Add eggs and yolk, one at a time, scraping down sides of bowl until completely incorporated. Add sour cream and vanilla. Beat mixture, scraping down sides of bowl, until smooth.

Pour mixture into prepared crust in ungreased 9-inch springform pan. Place on a cookie sheet. Bake until cake is firm around edge and center barely jiggles when tapped, about 45 minutes. Refrigerate for at least 8 hours or overnight to completely set before serving.

Graham Crust

1½ cups graham meal or crushed graham crackers
½ cup brown sugar
¾ cup melted butter

Mix all ingredients in bowl using your fingertips until well moistened. Press into bottom of a 9-inch springform pan.

Recipe courtesy of Eli's Cheesecake

CHICAGO-STYLE PIZZA PUFFS

izza Puffs are the smaller, deep-fried cousins of Chicago's deep dish pizza. Indigenous to Chicago's fast-food restaurants, these flaky, folded, tasty pockets are filled with melt-in-your-mouth mozzarella and marinara.

It appears that these mouthwatering puffs were invented by Chicago-based Iltaco Foods. Established in 1927, the (Il)linois (Ta)male (Co)mpany was originally known for its Chicago-style hot tamales, which it supplied to the pushcart vendors who operated in the financial district of Chicago and

Pizza Puffs are the smaller, deep-fried cousins of Chicago's deep dish pizza.

beyond. Soon, Iltaco branched out and began manufacturing other products, including chili and tacos, but it was its "Original" Pizza Puffs that put it on the map. Today, Iltaco Foods exclusively manufactures Pizza Puffs and supplies them to retail outlets and restaurants in Chicagoland and beyond.

Pizza Puffs were likely inspired by the traditional Italian calzone, an oven-baked filled pizza that's folded in half. The Pizza Puff sets itself apart by jumping into a deep fat fryer until golden and delicious. You can bake them, too, for twelve to fifteen minutes until toasted.

Chicago-Style Pizza Puffs

Premade pizza dough
Canola oil
1 cup shredded mozzarella cheese
1 cup pizza sauce
½ cup finely chopped pepperoni

Make pizza dough an hour or two ahead of time or use premade dough. Add ⅓ inch of oil to a fry pan and heat to 365° Fahrenheit. Roll out pizza dough on a floured surface into a ¼-inch-thick rectangle. Cut into about 20 smaller rectangles.

In a small bowl, mix together the cheese, sauce and pepperoni. Place 1 tablespoon dollops of the cheese, pepperoni and sauce mixture at the center of 10 of the rectangles. Lay the other 10 rectangles on top and apply a thin line of water to the edge of the dough. Press to seal, using a fork to crimp the edges of the dough together.

Check the oil temperature and carefully add the Pizza Puffs. Cook for 2 minutes, turn over and cook for 1 minute more. Remove to a paper towel–lined plate.

CHICAGO-STYLE OYSTERS

Chicago has a long-standing love affair with oysters. They were served at the elegant Lake House Hotel, Chicago's first fine dining establishment, opened in 1836 on Kinzie Street, where the Wrigley Building stands today The advent of the railroad—and, more specifically, the refrigerated rail car (1863)—fueled the East Coast oyster craze. "By the turn of the twentieth century, there were many large Oyster House Restaurants in Chicago serving several East Coast varieties of oysters to the city's growing sophisticated population," explains Steve LaHaie, senior vice president of the Shaw's Crab House Division of Chicago's Lettuce Entertain You Enterprises, Inc.

Rector's Oyster House, established at the corner of Clark and Monroe Streets in 1884, was perhaps Chicago's most successful seafood restaurant. It was so popular during its first year of operation that owner Charles E. Rector opened a second location with the added bonus of a billiard parlor in 1885 at the Exchange Building. In his novel *Sister Carrie* (1900), Theodore Dreiser described Rector's as the social hub of the city:

> *Rector's, with its polished marble walls and floor, its profusion of lights, its show of china and silverware, and, above all, its reputation as a resort for actors and professional men, seemed to him the proper place for a successful man to go…At Rector's he could always obtain this satisfaction for there one could encounter politicians, brokers, actors, some rich young "rounders" of the town, all eating and drinking amid a buzz of popular commonplace conversation.*

Chicago has a long-standing love affair with oysters. They were first served at the elegant Lake House Hotel, Chicago's first fine dining establishment, established in 1836 on Kinzie Street, where the Wrigley Building stands today. *Anjali Pinto.*

Leon Kientz, a chef at Rector's original Chicago location, included no fewer than twenty-eight oyster recipes in his 1906 tome *The Fish and Oyster Book*. Rector-style fried oysters are an over-the-top take on everybody's favorite bivalve mollusks, while so-called Chicago-Style Oysters are baked and easy enough for even the novice cook.

While after Prohibition their popularity in Chicago waned, Chicago's love affair with oysters has recently been rekindled. "Today, the oyster tradition has been revived in many Chicago restaurants and oyster bars," enthuses LeHaie. "What goes around comes around, and oysters are happening in a big way again in Chicago."

Rector's-Style Fried Oysters

From The Fish and Oyster Book *by Leon Kientz, published by the Hotel Monthly Press, which operated out of the Merchandise Mart, in 1906.*

Select a dozen medium-sized oysters. Season with salt and pepper and roll in cracker meal. Dip them in a batter made of 2 eggs, 1 teaspoon of Lea and Perrins sauce and 2 tablespoons of oyster liquor (the liquid that is naturally inside the oyster shell; bottled clam juice, bottled seafood broth or equal parts chicken broth and water can be used instead). After which, roll them in a preparation of finely cut crabmeat, as much finely cut lobster and a little fresh breadcrumbs. Mix all well together, shape them nicely and fry in dry pan with clarified butter to a nice color. When done, dress them on a hot platter and garnish with parsley and pieces of lemon.

Chicago-Style Oysters

Delaware oysters (a large East Coast variety)
Tabasco sauce
Grated parmesan cheese

Place oysters in shell or muffin tin top with two dashes of Tabasco and a generous sprinkling of parmesan cheese. Bake at 350° Fahrenheit for 10 minutes.

Recipe courtesy of Shaw's Crabhouse executive chef Arnulfo Tellez

CHICAGO-STYLE PĄCZKI

Though they were born in Poland in the Middle Ages, pączki (pronounced "poonch-key"), traditional Polish filled donuts symbolizing the start of Lent, are a beloved Fat Tuesday tradition in Chicago. Though pączki are available for one day only, Chicagoans love indulging in these deep-fried delights made of a rich yeast dough filled with a variety of inventive fruits and creams and sprinkled with powdered sugar.

In Poland, pączki are traditionally filled with stewed plum or wild rose hip jam; Chicago-Style Pączki take the fillings to another level altogether, piping in everything from passion fruit jelly to whiskey chocolate to PB&J. The more creative the better.

Delightful Pastries, a Polish-owned bakery in the northwest side neighborhood of Jefferson Park, cranks out over fifty thousand pączki for Fat Tuesday using a generations-old family recipe with both traditional and over-the-top Chicago-style fillings, which change from year to year. "Pączki are very much celebrated in Chicago," shares Delightful Pastries owner Dobra Bielinski. "With our huge Polish population in Chicago, our old world traditions are still so dearly celebrated. Pączki Day is on everyone's radar, whether or not they're from Poland. They're too delicious not to celebrate! This makes Pączki Day one of our busiest days in the bakery. Everyone arrives with a smile on their face, and most people are biting into a pączki before they even get out the door!"

Chicago-Style Pączki

2 packages active dry yeast
1 cup milk
½ cup sugar
6 eggs
1 teaspoon salt
¼ teaspoon lemon oil
½ teaspoon orange oil
½ cup rum or vodka
4½ cups flour
⅓ cup butter
Thick jam, custard or filling of choice
Powdered sugar for dusting

Mix yeast with milk and let sit for 10 minutes. Add sugar, eggs, salt, oils, vodka and flour. Slowly add the butter. Knead into a smooth ball. Let the dough to rest for 1 hour. Roll dough on a floured surface to about ¾-inch thickness. Cut out into 3-inch rounds using a cookie cutter or glass. Put 1 tablespoon of filling in the center of half the circles. Brush the edges with water and top with the remaining rounds. Seal the edges very well. Let the paczki ferment for 1 to 1½ hours. Cook in oil at 356° Fahrenheit. Dust with powdered sugar.

PB&J Filling
Place ½ teaspoon peanut butter and ½ teaspoon jelly in the center of half the circles.

Chocolate-Whiskey Buttercream Filling
2 sticks butter, softened
3 tablespoons whiskey
5 cups confectioners' sugar
¼ cup chocolate chips, melted and cooled
2 tablespoons heavy cream

Beat butter and whiskey with a hand mixer until light and creamy. Slowly add confectioners' sugar until fully incorporated. Beat in melted chocolate. Slowly add cream until frosting reaches desired consistency. Place 1 teaspoon of filling in the center of half the circles.

Recipe courtesy of Dobra Bielinski, Delightful Pastries

ROESER'S GERMAN CHOCOLATE CAKE

For so many Chicago families, a birthday wouldn't be a birthday without a cake from Roeser's Bakery on North Avenue. Since 1911, when John Roeser Sr. opened the doors of his American dream—a bakery filled with sugary delights—Roeser's has been a part of not just birthdays but also weddings, baby showers, graduations and holiday celebrations.

John Roeser arrived in Chicago from Germany in 1905 and began earning a living selling his homemade bread from his horse and cart, saving up his money to one day buy a brick-and-mortar bakery of his own. In 1911, he opened Roeser's Bakery at 3216 West North Avenue.

Roeser's stands as Chicago's oldest family-owned retail bakery. John Roeser Jr. began working at the bakery in 1936; John Roeser III began helping out in 1974. Today, the bakery is run by John Roeser IV. See if you can find the photo of John Roeser I standing proudly with his delivery horse and wagon at the corner of Chicago Avenue and Wells Street in the early 1900s that hangs in the bakery.

Roeser's is best known for its German chocolate cake, a moist, delicious dessert composed of devil's food chocolate sponge cake layered with a decadent pecan and coconut flake filling. Contrary to popular belief, German chocolate cake doesn't originate from Germany; rather, it originated in Dorchester, Massachusetts, where American chocolatier Samuel German formulated the baking chocolate used in his namesake recipe. Roeser's perfected the recipe here in Chicago, making the cake even more decadent. Roeser's version is not just filled but also covered with the pecan and coconut

Since 1911, when John Roeser Sr. opened the doors of his American dream—a bakery filled with sugary delights—Roeser's has been a part of not just birthdays but also weddings, baby showers, graduations and holiday celebrations. *Chelsea Gibson.*

flake crème. Chocolate fudge sauce oozes out of the top of the cake, and it's crowned with a swirl of whipped cream, miniature chocolate chips, chopped green pistachios and a maraschino cherry.

Roeser's Bakery is still packed with customers waiting in line to place or pick up orders for its celebrated German chocolate cake. "Our cakes are quite simply better than all the rest," shares John Roeser IV. "We use only the highest-quality ingredients on the market, bake our cakes fresh every morning and take the extra time to make our cakes the way they were made 'in the good old days.'"

Roeser's German Chocolate Cake

½ cup boiling water
4 ounces Baker's German sweet baking chocolate
 (1 square of baking chocolate is usually 1 ounce)
2 cups all-purpose flour

¼ cup cocoa
1 teaspoon baking soda
1 teaspoon salt
2 cups sugar
1 cup butter
4 large eggs, separated
1 teaspoon vanilla
1 cup buttermilk
Optional: miniature chocolate chips, chopped green
  pistachios, maraschino cherry

Preheat oven to 350° Fahrenheit. Grease two 9-inch cake pans with cooking spray or butter. Dust with flour and set aside.

In a large measuring cup, pour the boiling water over the baking chocolate. Stir until smooth and set aside. Add the flour, cocoa, baking soda and salt to a mixing bowl and set aside.

In a larger mixing bowl, beat the sugar and butter with a hand mixer on medium speed until light, about 3 minutes. Add the egg yolks, one at a time, then reduce mixer speed to low and add baking chocolate and vanilla. Add cocoa mixture and buttermilk.

In yet another separate mixing bowl, add the egg whites and beat on medium speed with the hand mixer until they form soft peaks, about 4 minutes. Fold into cake batter. Divide the cake batter equally between the cake pans. Bake for about 30 to 35 minutes, or until a wooden toothpick comes out clean. Cool the cakes in their cake pans for 5 minutes, then remove from pan to wire racks.

Prepare coconut pecan filling. Spread between layers and over top and sides. Top the cake with a dollop of whipped cream, a sprinkle of miniature chocolate chips or chopped green pistachios and a maraschino cherry.

Coconut Pecan Filling

⅓ cup butter
1 cup sugar
I can evaporated milk

3 egg yolks
1 cup coconut flakes
1 cup chopped fancy pecan pieces

Melt the butter and sugar. Add the evaporated milk and egg yolks and mix well. Cook for 20 minutes, stirring every 5 minutes. Add coconut flakes and mix well. Add pecans, mix until incorporated and pour into a bowl. The longer the pecans sit in the mix, the darker it will get. Keep the German Chocolate Cake refrigerated.

Recipe courtesy of John Roeser Jr.

FRANGO MINT CHOCOLATE CHEESECAKE

Once upon a time, cauldrons bubbled with rich chocolate on the thirteenth floor of Marshall Field's flagship department store on Chicago's great street, State Street. While most department stores smelled like fine perfumes or colognes, the warm smell of rich chocolate wafted through the elegant departments, a constant reminder of the decadent Frango Mints, Marshall Field's trademark chocolate mint truffles, that were being poured into their molds, cooled on giant marble slabs and packaged in their signature boxes. Produced in-house for seventy years, few things could make hearts flutter like a box of freshly handcrafted Frango Mints.

Frango Mints weren't technically born in Chicago. When Marshall Field's bought out the Frederick

Few things could make hearts flutter like a box of freshly handcrafted Frango Mints. *Frango Mints.*

& Nelson department store in Seattle in 1929, the secret recipe for its creamy, chocolate Franco Mints was an added bonus. Marshall Field's changed the Franco to Frango and refined the recipe in its in-house Candy Kitchens. Demand for the chocolates overwhelmed the small kitchens, however, and in 1999, production moved out to a larger-scale factory, where Frango Mints are still made today using the same secret recipe.

Today, more than one million pounds of Frango chocolates are sold each year. Year-round flavors—mint, dark mint, double chocolate, caramel, toffee, raspberry and dark chocolate—are always available alongside seasonal flavors, including candy cane in the winter and passion fruit in the summer. Frango Mint Chocolate Cheesecake is one of the Walnut Room's most popular desserts. You can find the mints on the seventh floor, near the Walnut Room, and on the Lower Level at the Macy's Visitor Information Center on State Street or online at macys.com.

Frango Mint Chocolate Cheesecake

Crust
30 chocolate cookie wafers, such as Nabisco Famous
   Chocolate Wafers
4 tablespoons unsalted butter (½ stick), melted and cooled

Filling
1½ pounds cream cheese (3 8-ounce packages),
   at room temperature
1 cup sugar
2 large eggs, at room temperature
⅓ cup heavy whipping cream
½ teaspoon vanilla extract
15 Frango Mint Chocolates (milk; 5½ ounces), chopped
   coarse (about 1 cup)

Topping
¼ teaspoon unflavored gelatin
1 tablespoon cold water
5 Frango Mint Chocolates (milk; 1 ounce), chopped fine
½ cup sour cream

Make the crust

Heat the oven to 350° Fahrenheit. Place cookies in food processor and process until the pieces are crumbled. Add the melted butter and continue to process until the crumbs are fine. Pour the crumb mixture into a springform pan, using the bottom of a cup or your fingers, and press firmly and evenly into the bottom. Bake for 10 minutes. Cool completely before filling.

Prep the filling

Mix cream cheese and sugar in food processor until well blended. Add the eggs one at a time. Add cream and vanilla extract. Add the melted Frango Mints. Blend until very smooth. Pour into a springform pan onto baked crust and bake at 350° Fahrenheit for about 35 minutes, until firm.

Make the Topping

In a small bowl, soften the gelatin in cold water. Transfer to a double boiler and stir over hot—not simmering—water until the gelatin is dissolved. Add the chopped Frango Mints and stir until melted. Remove the pan from the water and cool until tepid. Whisk the sour cream into the cooled chocolate mixture until blended. Spread the topping over the cheesecake. Cover with plastic wrap and refrigerate at least 4 hours. Remove the sides of the springform pan. Smooth the sides of the cake with a wet, hot knife.

This recipe is adapted from The Marshall Field's Cookbook

HENRICI'S COFFEE CAKE

Henrici's, though long gone, will forever be remembered as one of Chicago's oldest and finest restaurants. In his 1932 guide, *Dining in Chicago*, author John Drury pondered, "Is there a Chicagoan living, no matter how old, who does not remember Henrici's windows, ever since his mother first took him downtown as a child—those big windows, laden with tantalizing creations in birthday, wedding, and fruit cakes and, at Christmas time, those big English plum puddings?" Located in the heart of the Randolph Street theater district, Henrici's was famous for its slogan, "No Orchestral Din," and known for offering an elegant, quiet, gourmand-friendly refuge from booming Chicago.

Phillip Henrici, the son of Viennese restaurateurs, immigrated in 1864 to New York, where he began his career working as a baker's apprentice. He moved to Chicago in 1868, opening a small diner at 71 North State Street, where he served coffee, sandwiches and pastries, advertising, "All you can eat for a quarter." Three fried eggs cost fifteen cents; a slice of apple pie, five cents. Then came the Chicago Fire, destroying the diner—but not the dream. Henrici rebuilt, relocating the establishment several times—to 215 West Madison, then 184 West Madison and then 174 and 175 West Madison—before opening his enormous full-service restaurant, complete with a "delicacy department" available for catering private parties, a bubbling fountain in the second-floor dining area, pastry cases packed with sweet delicacies, a main kitchen in the basement and even a smoking room, at 71 West Randolph.

Mar - 8, 1948

HENRICI'S
ON RANDOLPH
Chicago
Established 1868

Henrici's, though long gone, will forever be remembered as one of Chicago's oldest and finest restaurants. In his 1932 guide, *Dining in Chicago*, author John Drury pondered, "Is there a Chicagoan living, no matter how old, who does not remember Henrici's windows, ever since his mother first took him downtown as a child—those big windows, laden with tantalizing creations in birthday, wedding, and fruit cakes and, at Christmas time, those big English plum puddings?" Menu from Henrici's on Randolph (1945). *New York Public Library Digital Archives.*

Inspired by the large-scale, sumptuous dining halls of his native Vienna, Henrici employed architect August Fielder, a native of Elbing, Germany, and designer of the grand Germania Club on the near North Side, to bring his namesake restaurant to life. Two hundred seats, which later expanded into eight hundred seats, welcomed politicians, celebrities (actors, vaudevillians, opera singers) and writers, including Theodore Drieser and Edna Ferber. As Drury described it in 1932, "Its atmosphere today is practically the same as it was in the days of hoop skirts and side-burns. It is like a bit of the Old World in the midst of modern American skyscrapers; a breath of Vienna, that brilliant capital of dining halls. ...This atmosphere remains today, like that of a cool retreat in the midst of hot, feverish modernism."

Henrici's became best known for its eclectic menu. Popular dishes from around the world—Russian tea, Spanish omelets, German pancakes, Maracaibo chocolate, Wiener schnitzel, Boston baked pork and beans, English mutton chops, steak tartar and Lyonnais potatoes—were all featured on the original 1894 bill of fare. Henrici's was also notable for its pastries, pies, pancakes, confections, cakes and, perhaps most popular of all, coffeecakes. Coffee was served Viennese style, with a small, individual pitcher filled with whipped cream on the side.

Sadly, Henrici's closed its doors in 1962 to make way for the Civic (Daley) Center, but it will always be remembered as one of Chicago's most brilliant restaurants.

A 1922 edition of *Baking Industry* magazine, published in Chicago, included a recipe for coffeecake à la Henrici, adapted below.

Henrici's Coffee Cake

3 cups bread flour
4½ teaspoons (2 packets) active dry yeast
⅓ cup sugar
Dash of mace
Pinch of salt
¾ cup water
½ cup milk
¼ cup butter
2 eggs
Grated rind of 1 lemon
Juice of 1 lemon

Topping

½ cup sugar

½ cup flour

½ cup slivered almonds

Grated rind of 1 lemon

¼ cup butter, melted

In large bowl, combine 1½ cups flour, yeast, sugar, mace and salt. In a saucepan, heat the water, milk and butter until butter begins to melt. Add to flour mixture. Add the eggs, one at a time. Blend at low speed until moistened. Beat for 3 minutes at medium speed. Add the lemon juice and rind. By hand, gradually stir in remaining flour to make a stiff batter. Spread in a greased 13- by 9-inch pan.

Prepare the topping by combining all the ingredients in a small bowl. Sprinkle the topping over dough. Cover the topped cake and let rise in a warm place for 1 hour. Bake at 375°F for 30 minutes, or until golden brown.

PULLMAN BREAD

The beauty of Pullman Bread lies not in its pillowy, delicate texture; slightly sweet flavor; or thin, almost nonexistent crust but rather in its shape: a precisely squared, compact sandwich loaf. That unique shape—and its name—also reveals its origin: its compactness and strict squareness made it a loaf that could be easily stacked and efficiently stored in the tiny galleys of Pullman dining cars, where food was cooked and stored.

George Pullman's empire began with an uncomfortable, overnight train ride from Buffalo to Westfield, New York, in the mid-1800s, an era when train travel was merely tolerated. He began dreaming up ways to bring comfort and luxury to the then miserable train passenger experience. He partnered with a powerful friend and formed a company that began building (and eventually operating) ultra-lux sleeper cars. To house his workers, Pullman founded a company town on Chicago's South Side, which he named after none other than himself.

Pullman's sleeper cars could best be described as five-star hotels rolling along on the rails. All the usual guest amenities were in place and the décor nothing less than opulent. Crystal chandeliers hung unshaken from the ceilings, while rubberized springs prevented the uncomfortable jiggling that had plagued train travel. Elegant, upholstered seats unfolded into comfortable berths. In the morning, silk shades were drawn, allowing passengers to gaze on the sun-blessed, still so untouched landscape of a fast-growing America.

Pullman's dining cars were known for their exceptional cuisine. Raw oysters, roast spring lamb with mint sauce, fricandeau of veal à la macedoine,

The beauty of Pullman Bread lies not in its pillowy, delicate texture; slightly sweet flavor; or thin, almost nonexistent crust, but rather in its shape: a precisely squared, compact sandwich loaf that could be easily stacked and efficiently stored in the tiny galleys of Pullman dining cars. *Wikimedia.*

venison steaks and lobster salad were among the menu choices, all served with the finest wines, champagnes, whiskeys, brandies, beers and ales from around the world. Sublime service was provided by the Pullman porters, African American men who fought hard for respect, formed the first black labor union and were an integral part of the passenger railroad industry.

Pullman Bread was inspired by the French pain de mie, a name that loosely translates to crustless bread. The Pullman company, however, invented the special metal baking pans with their sliding lids, adapting the recipe to American tastes and creating the fitting shape that worked well for rail transport. This yeasted, fine white bread with its symmetrical slices is ideal for sandwiches or toasting.

Pullman Bread

You'll need a lidded Pullman pan to make Pullman Bread; you can easily find and order one online.

1 cup lukewarm water
⅔ cup milk plus ¼ cup milk, room temperature
6 tablespoons butter, melted and cooled
2 teaspoons salt
3 tablespoons honey
5 cups bread flour
2 teaspoons instant yeast

In a large mixing bowl, combine the water, milk, butter, salt and honey. Stir in the flour and yeast. Knead the dough on a lightly greased surface until smooth. Let the dough rise until doubled in size, about 1 to 2 hours. Knead the dough for a second time and shape into a log.

Preheat your oven to 350° Fahrenheit. Lightly grease your Pullman loaf pan, remembering to grease the interior top of the slide-off lid as well. The dough loaf should fill about ⅓ of the pan so that it will bake to the top, creating a perfectly squared loaf. Bake the bread for 25 minutes at the center of the oven. Remove the bread from the oven and carefully slide off the lid, return to the oven and bake for another 15 minutes.

CHICAGO-STYLE RIB TIPS

Chicago-Style Rib Tips are a reminder of our past status as the "hog butcher of the world." These fatty, short leftovers from trimmed spare ribs were once tossed out by butchers. Yet when seasoned, rubbed, slow grilled and served over hand-cut fries, smothered in their signature spicy, vinegary sauce, with slices of white Wonder bread to sop up the smoky juices, they transform into something altogether sublime.

Chicago makes its mark on the barbecue map of excellence thanks to both old-school and trendy BBQ hotspots, where four distinct styles of barbecue make mouths water from the North to the South Sides. Boilbecue, a technique that calls for boiling ribs in a cabbage, onion, potato and caraway-infused broth, was introduced at the turn of the century by Eastern European immigrants. Modern barbecue calls for slowly roasted meats with a little help from controlled technology—specifically, gas ovens. Fusion barbecue applies modern techniques and out-of-the-ordinary flavors to exotic cuts. Delta barbecue harnesses the power of the open pit or the equally labor-intensive, only-in-Chicago aquarium cooker, after which they're doused with a sauce that falls between mild and spicy with an added, tangy kick. Chicago-style rib tips fall in this fourth category.

Black farmers from the Mississippi Delta packed their barbecue genius as they moved to Chicago in search of higher-paying factory jobs during second Great Migration that lasted from 1940 to 1970. In the 1950s, a genius by the name of Leo Davis created the first aquarium smoker in his sheet metal shop after city restaurant inspectors began cracking down on open pits. Aquarium cookers were also easier to clean, though they re-created the open

Chicago-Style Rib Tips are a reminder of our past status as the "hog butcher of the world." These fatty, short bits—leftovers from trimmed spare ribs—were once tossed out by butchers. *New York Public Library Digital Archives.*

pit cooking method and are meant to be fired up with wood (though some masters use charcoal or a mixture of wood and charcoal). Their tempered glass doors—which give off the impression that its really a sort of aquarium—were perfect for displaying drool-worthy barbecue, and not exotic fish, while keeping the goods warm, moist and ready to eat. Just like with open-pit barbecuing, the aquarium cooker needs a master at its helm. Maintaining the 190- to 225-degree Fahrenheit temperature range is an art in and of itself.

Chicago-Style Rib Tips start out as just another cheap cut of meat. But with a little patience, skill and a lot of artistry, they transform into an iconic Chicago dish that manages to be both humble and extraordinary.

Chicago-Style BBQ Rib Tips

4 pounds pork rib tips

Rub
¼ cup light brown sugar
2 tablespoons seasoned salt
1 tablespoon chili powder
2 teaspoons ground black pepper

1 teaspoon paprika
1 teaspoon cayenne
1 teaspoon dried sage
1 teaspoon onion powder
1 teaspoon garlic powder
1 teaspoon Old Bay seasoning

Make the rub by mixing all the spices together. Rub the rib tips with the spice mixture and let sit for 1 hour while you make the sauce.

Sauce

⅓ cup ketchup
⅓ cup pineapple juice
¼ cup dark brown sugar
2 tablespoons apple cider vinegar
1 teaspoon Tabasco
1 tablespoon chili powder
1 teaspoon dry mustard
2 tablespoons Worcestershire sauce
1 teaspoon seasoned salt
1 teaspoon black pepper
½ teaspoon garlic powder
½ teaspoon onion powder
½ teaspoon ground celery seed

In a medium-sized saucepan over low heat, stir the ketchup, pineapple juice, sugar, vinegar, Tabasco, chili powder, dry mustard, Worcestershire sauce, seasoned salt, pepper, garlic powder, onion powder and ground celery seed. Cook, stirring occasionally, for 30 minutes, until thickened.

Rib Tips

Immerse large wood chips of choice in water for 30 minutes. Fire up your grill to low heat (250° to 300°Fahrenheit). Toss the wood chips on the coal briquettes. Brush and oil the grill grate. Arrange the tips on the hot grate. Cover the grill and cook for approximately 3 hours, replenishing coal briquettes as necessary to maintain an even, low temperature. Brush with sauce and continue cooking until tender.

Serve over hand-cut French fries, with a slice or two (or three) of Wonder Bread to soak up the tangy sauce.

GREEN RIVER SODA

Sweet, sour and fluorescent, Green River is a soda born and raised in Chicago. This fizzy Prohibition baby recalls soda fountains and St. Patrick's. It has inspired hit songs and has quashed the thirst of countless Chicago kids.

Green River was invented by the Schoenhofen Brewery, brewers of the popular Edelweiss beer, established in Chicago in the 1850s. When Prohibition hit, the company survived by focusing on near bear and soda pop. Green River, born in 1919, helped Schoenhofen limp along through Prohibition until it closed completely in 1950. Other manufacturers copied the recipe, and the soda's popularity carried on. You can still spot the Schoenhofen Brewery's powerhouse and administrative buildings, located at Eighteenth and Canalport. Look for hexagrams—the Brewer's Star, symbolizing purity—on the façades; indeed, the brewery sits on a still pure, ancient aquifer.

Green River flowed through soda fountains across the United States in syrup form and was especially popular in the Midwest. The green syrup inspired John Fogerty of Creedence Clearwater Revival to pen the song (and album) "Green River," released in 1969. In a 1993 *Rolling Stone* interview, Fogerty explained that Green River is

> *really about this place where I used to go as a kid on Putah Creek, near Winters, California. I went there with my family every year until I was ten. Lot of happy memories there. I learned how to swim there. There was*

Above: Sweet, sour and fluorescent, Green River is a soda born and raised in Chicago. *John Wondrasek.*

Right: Green River was invented by the Schoenhofen Brewery, established in Chicago in the 1850s and brewers of the popular Edelweiss Beer. Retro ad for Green River. *John Wondrasek.*

Green River, born in 1919, helped Schoenhofen Brewery limp along through Prohibition until it closed completely in 1950. *John Wondrasek.*

a rope hanging from the tree. Certainly dragonflies, bullfrogs. There was a little cabin we would stay in owned by a descendant of Buffalo Bill Cody. That's the reference in the song to Cody Jr. The actual specific reference, Green River, I got from a soda pop syrup label. You used to be able to go into a soda fountain, and they had these bottles of flavored syrup. My flavor was called Green River. It was green, lime flavored, and they would empty some out over some ice and pour some of that soda water on it, and you had yourself a Green River.

To make your own old-fashioned soda fountain–style phosphate Green River, you'll need acid phosphate, a tart, tongue-tingling solution with the same pH as freshly squeezed lime juice.

Green River Soda

4 tablespoons Green River Syrup
12 ounces carbonated water (1½ cup)
1 teaspoon acid phosphate

Stir all the ingredients into a glass and add ice.

Green River Syrup
2 limes, sliced
2 lemons, sliced
2 cups sugar
2 cups water

Add all the ingredients to a sauce pan and bring to a boil. Boil gently for 5 minutes, stirring occasionally. Remove from heat and let cool. Strain into a glass storage container.

TWINKIES

Twinkies are more than everybody's quintessential junk food treat; they're also an iconic guilty pleasure, the stuff of urban legends. These "forever fresh" spongy snack cakes have been packed into countless lunchboxes, deep fried at county fairs, stockpiled in nuclear bomb shelters and sealed in time capsules. When they disappeared from store shelves in 2012 after their parent company, Hostess, filed for Chapter 11 bankruptcy protection, Twinkie fans went berserk. The golden, mini submarine–shaped cakes (they're affectionately called *submarinos* in Spanish) eventually began rolling down the production line again, to the tune of over one million Twinkies per day.

Twinkies were invented as a solution to a seasonal problem. The Continental Baking Company, located in the near northwest Chicago suburb of Schiller Park, was known for making delicious strawberry shortcakes. But strawberry season lasts from only mid-April through June, and the shortcake machinery stood idle for the rest of the year. In 1931, baker and factory manager James Alexander Dewar came up with a solution: at the end of strawberry season, he began baking the shortcakes into small canoes and filling them with banana cream. Bananas are available year round, unlike strawberries While on a business trip to St. Louis, Dewar passed a billboard for a shoe company called the "Twinkle Toe Shoe Co." A light bulb went off, and Twinkies were officially born. Sold in pairs for just a nickel, they were an almost instant success.

When bananas were rationed during World War II, banana cream was replaced with the vanilla cream of today. By the 1950s, Twinkies had become

Twinkies are more than everybody's quintessential junk food treat; they're also an iconic guilty pleasure, the stuff of urban legends. *Wikimedia.*

a lunchbox staple thanks to their sponsorship of the wildly popular *Howdy Doody Show*. In the 1970s, Twinkie the Kid, the Twinkie-shaped, ten gallon hat–wearing mascot, galloped into town promising "A Big Delight in Every Bite."

Urban legend has it that Twinkies really do stay fresh forever; indeed, Twinkies were once bomb shelter staples, together with canned goods, and President Clinton even hopefully placed a package in a time capsule at the National Archives (though it was later removed due to fears of a potential mice infestation).

"Twinkies were the best darn tootin' idea I ever had," an eighty-three-year-old Dewar shared in a *Chicago Tribune* interview on the fiftieth anniversary of the Twinkie. "I still eat at least three of them a day."

Twinkies

This recipe re-creates the original Twinkie, made with banana cream filling. Your best bet is to buy a cream canoe cake/éclair pan and cake cream pastry injector, but you can also make do with a cupcake tin and a pastry bag fitted with a medium tip.

2 cups sifted all-purpose flour

1½ cups sugar

1 tablespoon baking powder

1 teaspoon salt

½ cup vegetable oil

7 egg yolks

¾ cup cold water

2 teaspoons vanilla

2 to 3 teaspoons grated lemon or orange peel

1 cup egg whites (about 7)

½ teaspoon cream of tartar

Preheat oven to 325° Fahrenheit. Sift the flour, sugar, baking powder and salt into a large mixing bowl. Make a well and add oil, egg yolks, water, vanilla and citrus peel. Beat with hand mixer on low speed until smooth.

In a separate bowl, beat the egg whites with the cream of tartar until stiff peaks form. Very gently fold the egg yolk mixture into the egg whites until blended.

Pour the batter into a well-greased canoe cake pan. Bake until the tops of the cake are just barely golden, about 15 minutes. Allow the cakes to cool before filling.

Banana Filing

½ stick sweet butter, room temperature (2 ounces)

⅛ teaspoon salt

½ cup mashed bananas

3 cups sifted confectioners sugar

Cream butter and salt. Add the bananas. Gradually add the sugar. Beat until fluffy. To fill your Twinkies, transfer the frosting to a pastry bag with a small tip. Poke three holes in the bottom of the Twinkie and carefully pipe the frosting through each hole and into the center, being careful not to overfill.

PORTILLO'S CHOCOLATE CAKE

Dick Portillo opened his first fast-food stand in 1963, quickly developing a reputation for the best of the best hot dogs, Italian beef sandwiches, burgers and even salads. A long line of cars waits patiently at the drive-through for a bite of Portillo's goods. But the iconic icing on the cake is Portillo's ultra-rich, moist, to-die-for chocolate cake. It's been the centerpiece of anniversaries, picnics, graduations, birthday bashes, baby showers, breakups and plain old everyday parties of one. Grab a fork and take a bite into this luscious chocolaty cake and you'll understand why.

Dick Portillo started his empire when he poured a whopping $1,100 into the small trailer sans bathroom or running water that became the first Portillo's hot dog stand in Villa Park. He affectionately named it the Dog House. Fifty-two years and thirty-eight locations later, Portillo's is officially out of the doghouse. It has become such a Chicago favorite that its goods—including the famous chocolate cake—can be overnighted via UPS anywhere in the United States, including Hawaii and Alaska.

While the coveted Portillo's chocolate cake recipe remains top secret, a few foodies have cracked the code to understanding what makes it stand so far above the rest. It all boils down to the secret ingredient: mayonnaise. And as for the cake batter and rich chocolate frosting, Portillo's relies on good old Betty Crocker. Light, moist, tender and not cloyingly sweet, this is a cake you'll want to serve for your next big or little celebration.

Portillo's Chocolate Cake

1 Betty Crocker devil's food cake mix
3 eggs
1 cup water
1 cup mayonnaise
2 cans Betty Crocker chocolate frosting

Preheat oven to 350° Fahrenheit. Grease 2 round cake pans.

Beat the first 4 ingredients for about 4 minutes or until fluffy. Pour into prepared pans. Bake for about 30 minutes, or until a toothpick inserted into the middle comes out clean.

Let cakes cool for 1 hour. Plate one cake and frost with about ¾ can of Betty Crocker chocolate frosting. Set the second cake on top of the first cake and frost the top and sides with the remaining frosting.

MORTON'S BAKED FIVE-ONION SOUP

Caramelized onions; a rich, slightly sweet, savory broth; a thick slice of toasted French bread; and melty Jarlsberg cheese are the hallmarks of French onion soup. Morton's Steakhouse takes the classic soup five steps further by adding four onions, plus one wild onion—garlic—creating a slightly sweet and savory broth. Morton's Five-Onion Soup is the perfect prelude to the steakhouse's roasted prime rib, New York strip steak or filet mignon. It's also guaranteed to keep vampires at a distance.

Though they both grew up in Chicago, both the sons of restaurateurs Arnie Morton and Klaus Fritsch met at the Playboy Club in Montreal. After working as Hugh Hefner's right-hand man, Morton brought glitz and glamour to Chicago's Gold Coast, opening restaurants and even a luxe nightclub, all of which helped establish the area as a dining and entertainment hub. The duo opened the original Morton's Steakhouse in a Gold Coast high rise in 1978, and it instantly became a celebrity hotspot.

Morton's sublime Baked Five-Onion Soup celebrates the humble onion, Chicago's namesake.

Morton's Baked Five-Onion Soup

1 tablespoon olive oil
2 large Spanish onions, thinly sliced
1 large red onion, thinly sliced
1 small leek, halved, thinly sliced and well rinsed
4 shallots, thinly sliced
¼ cup minced garlic (about 20 cloves)
5 tablespoons dry sherry
¼ cup Madeira wine
8 cups beef broth
1 teaspoon fresh thyme leaves
¼ teaspoon herbs de Provence
1 bay leaf
1 teaspoon salt
½ teaspoon freshly ground white pepper
Loaf of crusty French bread, sliced and toasted
1 cup Jarlsberg cheese, grated
¼ cup fresh chives, chopped

Heat the olive oil over medium-low heat in a large (6-quart) soup pot; add both types of onions, the leek, shallots and garlic and cook, stirring frequently, for 30 to 35 minutes or until onions are softened and a deep golden brown.

Add the sherry, Madeira, beef broth, thyme, herbs de Provence and bay leaf. Simmer, partially covered, for about 20 minutes.

Preheat the broiler. Remove the bay leaf, adjust the seasoning with salt and pepper and ladle the soup into broiler-safe soup crocks. Lay a toasted bread slice on top of each soup and generously sprinkle with cheese. Broil for about 2 minutes, until the cheese browns and the soup bubbles around the sides. Garnish with chopped fresh chives and serve immediately.

Recipe adapted from one featured in Morton's The Cookbook: 100 Steakhouse Recipes for Every Kitchen *by Klaus Fitsch*

AKUTAGAWA

Akutagawa is a dish born of the Japanese American community that thrived in Lakeview after World War II. Wok-scrambled eggs, minced onions and your choice of beef sausage or chicken are garnished with chopped green peppers and bean sprouts, served with a side of white rice and graciously topped with American-style Sunday dinner gravy. It's a stick-to-your-ribs, belly-warming, hangover-curing dish best eaten at a diner counter with a cup of joe.

In a 2015 episode of Chicago Public Radio's *Afternoon Shift* program devoted to Lakeview's Japanese American community, area resident Emi Yamauchi shared recollections with host Niala Boodhoo. Of culinary note were her fond memories of the her father's restaurant, Hamburger King, a popular Lakeview diner that offered American fare with Japanese flair:

> *Except for the hamburgers and grilled cheese, just about everything on the menu could be ordered with rice—Polish sausage, eggs and rice; bacon and eggs and rice; flank steak and rice; pork chops and rice; chili mac and rice; and of course, rice and gravy...The "famous" special dish* [was] *called the Akutagawa, after George Akutagawa, who was a frequent customer. This was his favorite dish. It consisted of ground hamburger, bean sprouts, eggs and onions all mixed together on a flat-top grill and served with rice.*

Today, Hamburger King has morphed into another diner, Rice N'Bread, yet 2435 North Sheffield remains a place where you can satisfy late night and

Akutagawa is a dish born of the Japanese American community that thrived in Lakeview after World War II. It's still one of the most popular menu items at Rice N'Bread, formerly Hamburger King (3435 North Sheffield Avenue). *Rice N'Bread.*

early bird cravings with a diner menu like no other. Bulgogi and burgers, dak dak and Denver omelets, pancakes and kimchee all coexist happily on both the menu and the plate. Akutagawa remains on the menu, too. "The customers love Akutagawa," shares the current owner, Mr. L. Park. "We kept it on our menu out of tradition, and it remains one of our most popular dishes."

Akutagawa

6 links of pork sausage
6 eggs
2 tablespoons milk
½ cup minced onion
2 tablespoons soy sauce
½ teaspoon black pepper
1 tablespoon butter

½ cup bean sprouts
¼ cup chopped green peppers

Cook sausage over medium-high heat in a wok until evenly brown. Drain and chop into bite-size pieces. Set aside.

Whisk together the eggs, milk, onions, soy sauce and black pepper in a large bowl. Melt the butter in the wok over medium to high heat. Stir in eggs and continue stirring until they have just cooked.

Garnish with bean sprouts and chopped green peppers. Serve with a side of white rice. Top with a generous pour of quick gravy.

Quick Gravy

1 tablespoon butter
2 tablespoons all-purpose flour
¼ teaspoon Old Bay seasoning
Pinch of salt and pepper
1 cup beef broth

Melt butter in a small saucepan over medium heat. Add flour, Old Bay seasoning, salt and pepper, stirring with a whisk. Gradually add broth, stirring until blended. Cook 2 minutes or until thick, stirring constantly.

RECOMMENDED READING
AND EATING

While you can make all of these recipes at home, these iconic dishes, drinks and desserts are best enjoyed in the historic places where they were born. Of special note are Bertha Palmer's Brownies at the Lobby Bar in the historic Palmer House (17 East Monroe Street), Bookbinder Soup at the Drake Hotel's Cape Cod Room (140 East Walton Street) and Mrs. Herring's Chicken Pot Pie at the Walnut Room (111 South State Street, seventh floor). One of the best places in the city to bite into a hot dog is at the Vienna Beef Factory employee cafeteria (2501 North Damen Avenue)—open to the public—where you can count on just-encased hot dogs served by the pros. Pick up a delectable Andersonville Coffee Cake at the Swedish Bakery (5348 North Clark) or a dozen boxed cinnamon rolls from Ann Sather's (909 West Belmont) for your next breakfast bonanza. Order a customized Roeser's German Chocolate Cake (3616 West North Avenue) or an original Eli's Cheesecake (6701 Forest Preserve Drive) for your next birthday bash. Cool off on a hot summer night with an Italian Lemonade at Mario's Italian Lemonade (1066 West Taylor Street), a Rainbow Cone at Original Rainbow Cone (9233 South Western Avenue) or an Atomic Sundae at Margie's Candies (1960 North Western Avenue).

Pack a picnic of sandwiches made with slices of Pullman Bread and enjoy a day at the Pullman National Monument (11141 South Cottage Grove Avenue). You can learn more recipes that were likely served in Pullman's moving palaces in Rufus Estes' *Good Things to Eat* (1911). Estes was a railway chef for the Pullman Company and is considered the first African American chef to publish a cookbook.

A handful of iconic Chicago restaurants have published cookbooks of their very own, including *Marshall Field's Cookbook* (2006), *Morton's the Cookbook* (2009) and *The Bergoff Family Cookbook* (2007).

John Drury's *Dining in Chicago* (1931) will take you on a journey through Chicago's storied post-Prohibition restaurant landscape, while Herbert Asbury brings old Chicago and its underworld to life in *Gem of the Prairie* (1940).

Any top-notch Chicago bartender will serve the classic cocktails—minus the Mickey Finn—upon request. For more classic cocktails, refer to *The Ideal Bartender* by Tom Bullock (1917), *The Savoy Cocktail Book* (1930) or *The Old Waldorf-Astoria Bar Book* (1934).

ABOUT THE AUTHOR

Amy Bizzarri is an extreme Chicago history buff and freelance writer. She lives with her two children in a vintage 1910 home in the Logan Square neighborhood of Chicago. When she's not writing, you'll most likely find her swimming laps at Holstein Park pool, riding her bicycle around Humboldt Park or sharing an Atomic Sundae at Margie's Candies. Amy blogs at DiscoveringVintageChicago.com.

Photo courtesy of Vavoom Pinups.

Visit us at
www.historypress.net
....
This title is also available as an e-book